THE POLYAMORY PARADOX

FINDING YOUR CONFIDENCE IN CONSENSUAL NON-MONOGAMY

IRENE MORNING

Difference Press

Washington, DC, USA

Published 2022

DISCLAIMERS

Editing: Natasa Smirnov

Author's photo courtesy of: Lindsay Keys

ADVANCE PRAISE

"Most early explorers must tackle the triple challenge of learning and integrating new ways of being, unlearning deeply conditioned values and beliefs about how adults should relate to one another, all while navigating the turbulent landscape of their own (and often at least one partner's) attachment wounds.

The Polyamory Paradox brilliantly, accessibly, and compassionately explains these challenges and offers clear strategies for accessing the joy, pleasure, connection, and transformation that can be found through ethical nonmonogamy. This isn't head-in-the-clouds theory or pushing a polemical point of view about how ENM should work. Irene meets readers where they are and takes them on a journey of understanding their own emotional landscapes that, for many, will end in greater freedom, flexibility, and self-compassion.

In my estimation, Irene has written perhaps the finest practical guide to navigating the specific socioemotional pitfalls of transitioning from compulsory monogamy to non-monogamous practice I've seen. It's sure to be an instant classic in the field."

— WILLIAM WINTERS, SEX & RELATIONSHIP
COACH AND FOUNDER/CO-ORGANIZER OF
BONOBO NETWORK

"This book will be extremely helpful for those who are both new to polyamory and ethical non-monogamy and for those who are more experienced. The challenges that are faced often have to do with jealousy, time, capacity, and matched (or mis-matched) poly styles. This book will help the reader navigate through these topics to learn more about themselves and indirectly help them get clearer on what type of traits would be a good match for them and potential poly partners."

— ERIN TILLMAN, CSE, CERTIFIED SEX
EDUCATOR, INTIMACY COORDINATOR &
EXECUTIVE DIRECTOR OF SEX-POSITIVE LA

"A bold and honest journey and guide about the beautiful healing that can come from opening up. Irene has created a wonderful trauma-informed guide to being perfectly imperfect in relationships. With her personable style, you feel held and seen by Irene as she walks alongside you in healing through relationships."

— NICOLETTA HEIDEGGER, MA, MED, LMFT,
SEX THERAPIST & HOST OF SLUTS AND
SCHOLARS

"This was read one out of 100 for me... The dark doesn't feel as lonely and the light feels more accessible with commitment to listening to our bodies, learning about ourselves, and generating agency that is long overdue for so many of us."

— KIKI LEDERER, PLEASURE WITCH

CONTENTS

For Eileen

WHEN OPENING UP FEELS LIKE FALLING APART

"I just don't even know if I'm poly. I think maybe I'm sexually open, but I can't handle the emotional attachment stuff here. We're going to have to break up. I'm just spinning out," Rhiannon says to me after her first meeting with the new metamour (for those who don't speak non-monogamy, that means partner of your partner). She had called her partner a couple of weeks prior and was startled to have him answer the phone while on a date with this other woman, Ana. He had talked to Rhiannon about this budding relationship, but she didn't know when and where, and how he would be seeing the new metamour. The surprise of hearing his voice on the end of the line mid-connection with someone else set off internal alarm bells. It was as though her mind was saying, "OK, big emotions! You're up!" but her body just kind of went numb.

She proceeds to describe how, more recently, a minor miscommunication landed her in her partner's house after a night of no sleep, face-to-face with her partner's new love interest. She knew she wasn't ready to meet this woman, but her guard was down, and it felt like that was just the way the cookie was going to crumble. He was soundly sleeping in the other room while the two women made an effort with each other. "Of course, the guy here just conks out in the midst of a sensitive situation." They are able to roll their eyes together at the wonder that is the uncanny, always-accessible slumber of a man unencumbered by any form of systemic oppression. "I mean, this woman was nice enough," Rhiannon explains. "She's not my cup of tea, but we can get along just fine, and I know cognitively that I'm still primary. But it's like suddenly my body has no idea what that means to him."

The morning after this accidental meeting, she and her partner spent hours processing and doing repair work around the rupture created in their relationship. She left his house to run an errand, and when she called shortly thereafter to check in, Ana was back at his house. From this point, Rhiannon's body flew off the handle. "I just don't understand how that could be his move so quickly after all the processing we had done. Like, give me a minute to regroup. It just feels like throwing another log on the flame when I'm saying I need to put the fire out. How could he think I would be OK with that? Also like, I just left! You can't be alone for five minutes?"

Then she says what I hear from nearly all my non-monogamous clients in the peak of disconnection, "It's like he doesn't know me. He can't see me the way I thought he did." (To be fair, this is a feeling experienced in monogamy as well.)

Rhiannon is one of my clients who, after her divorce, looked around her community and saw close friends and people she admired in seemingly more fulfilling relationships than the marriage she had dissolved. From the outside, these relationships looked happy and exciting and full of pleasure and sexual expansion. Most of what she was seeing were long-term open relationships, and the thing that stood out most was that the existing couple seemed so connected to each other. She thought to herself, "Hey, the traditional way had its issues. Maybe there's something to pursuing polyamory."

Fast forward to eighteen months later and this client has shed her body shame, is having great sex with multiple partners, dating various people with varying degrees of experience in non-monogamy, and all around living her best life. Enter Eric, who becomes the first person she actually falls in love with as this new, transformed version of herself. He has been in sexually liberated spaces for a couple of decades and fits right into the lifestyle she's been cultivating. In addition to beautiful dates and deepening intimacy, group sex and swinger resorts are all on the table. He is pretty clear that he is looking to have a primary partner (term used in mostly hierarchical non-monogamy to designate the relationship that tends to get more resources and priority) with whom he can build the rest of his life and be deeply emotionally bonded, while simultaneously continuing to embody his personal values of sexual freedom and erotic expression. They discuss being each other's primary partners. And so it is, for several earth-shakingly beautiful months.

As is to be expected, my client finds the conjoining of sexual liberation and emotional attachment truly awe-inspiring. She is in love, and everything is thrilling. That is, until he starts developing an emotional attachment to someone else. Where our sessions had been mostly focused on receiving all the good, abundant, juicy amazingness, suddenly we were working to contain anxiety attacks and bring back normalcy to sleep and appetite. The same way we sometimes lose sleep and hunger when we're falling in love, our body sometimes does this when someone we're in love with is falling in love. Except in this case, we don't have our own happy hormones to make us not care.

Non-monogamy is not for the faint of heart. It challenges the majority of our social conditioning, most of which we're not even aware of until we are forced to confront it. It lays bare even the tiniest of cracks in our existing partnerships as they begin to open up. It reveals our limits and our misalignments in relationships that develop with some level of openness from the beginning. Whether you are opening an existing relationship or making your personal transition in the context of a new relationship, it will hit upon the places where you are still wounded and find a way to rub salt in them.

Noa thought about his open relationship in a similar way; he came to me wanting support with becoming the strong anchor his long-distance partner needed while she dove headfirst into the deep-end of a new, sex-positive life in her fifties. They were mostly long-distance, and she was going to play parties and tantra workshops with other people in other cities. When they were together, everything was blissful and amazing. When they weren't, he was falling apart. He was losing weight and feeling sick to his stomach all the time. In his view, he needed to step into the role of a man who could offer her a strong foundation from which to explore all this newfound freedom. He wanted to relinquish his desire for regular phone calls because she was adopting more of a "we'll talk when we can" attitude, and he didn't want to hinder her in any way. When they went to parties together, he would spend the night with the sensation of chasing her around, feeling a duty to protect her.

Going to sex parties – or even regular parties where one partner might want to peel off with someone else –

can be even more triggering than being apart because the trigger is more immediately in front of your face. What happens when your partner connects with someone to whom you don't really feel drawn, and they want to have some time together? What happens when you go with them to try to step outside your comfort zone, but you internally freak out watching your partner touch someone else? What happens when you're right there with them, but the dynamic hasn't been discussed ahead of time and they wind up having sex without you?

Sound familiar? If you're new to polyamory, you've likely mulled over some of these questions. Unless you happen to be blessed with a rich community of sex-positive, polyamorous folks who are a couple steps ahead of you, chances are you don't have any role models for this. It's also highly likely that in the midst of a rupture-inspired meltdown, a friend will say something like, "I don't know how you do it. I could never."

For me and many of the folks I work with, this lack of understanding from our inner circle makes us even more on edge. When you're confused, feeling hurt, and probably even a little ashamed, having to gauge whether or not a friend is going to be able to hold space for you becomes a stressor you don't want to add to the mix. The result can be withdrawing inward even further in an ongoing crisis, which, unfortunately, doesn't help.

From the outside, people might assume that being non-monogamous is full of fun and sex and always feeling connected to people since you can have multiple relationships. On the inside, it can be overwhelmingly triggering and painfully lonely as evident from the examples above.

A lot of the relationship advice I have for non-monogamous people is also true for monogamous people, but non-monogamy often shoves the reason for that advice in your face with a lot more oomph! In trying to be open and move through our discomfort, we can find ourselves in situations we simply didn't anticipate, stirring up pain points we didn't realize course so deeply.

There are maybe a couple of people in the world for whom transitioning from monogamy to non-monogamy *ain't no thang*. Those people, I imagine, are polyamorous as part of their identity, and likely either grew up in families or communities that had an open attitude toward non-monogamy and / or figured out very early on how to prioritize their own knowing and needs above any external expectations placed on them. Most of us are not those people.

Because the full spectrum of non-monogamy is not really reflected in our broader culture or mainstream media, we have many, many misperceptions about it. I've lost count of how many guys have expressed to me some version of "I just want my girlfriend to find it hot when I sleep with other women" when they run into speedbumps opening up. Sure, a hetero-passing couple slipping right into a dynamic like that is possible, but it requires certain relational elements to make it secure. And as Jessica Fern tells us in *Polysecure*, monogamous relationships are often relying simply on the structure of the relationship for that security, not the actual *quality* of the intimacy (not all, but most who have gotten along OK with monogamy being the default).

Compulsory monogamy culture (mononormativity) is a societal and cultural context that assumes monogamous romantic and sexual relationships to be the norm, and also the most beneficial to society. The culture that comes with this default imbues values that emphasize the importance of the monogamous couple above other ways of being. Some of that conditioning can take the form of expecting self-sacrifice, external validation playing a big role in the relationship, expectation for the partner to fill every need you have, tying self-worth to partnership status, putting the romantic relationship above all else, overcoming incompatibility with the power of true love, "the one," etc. Some people refer to this as "toxic monogamy." And because humans are social creatures who depend upon social relationships for survival, this conditioning impacts us on a very deep level, rippling into how we operate in various realms of our lives, not just intimate relationships.

In addition to monogamous relationships being a default in our culture, we also swim in the waters of compulsory heterosexuality. I know I'm not the only one who heard, "I bet the boys really like you," or "Which boy do you have a crush on?" before I was old enough to have established my own relationship with desire. The assumptions voiced by those around us and the representations that dominate our media exposure shape our understanding of what is socially acceptable. For those who know they are queer, or who at least have an inkling, this can cause a great deal of pain and suffering. Living in a culture in which you are forced to declare yourself as "other" (i.e., the process of coming out) is traumatizing for most, deadly at its worst, and not fully supportive at its best. Beyond those who have clarity about their queerness, and because human sexuality is actually, overall, incredibly fluid in its nature and physiology, many of us find ourselves going along with the dominant projection of sexuality just because it works "well enough" for us. This is also an expression of us being disconnected from our bodies: we train ourselves from a young age not to notice or lean into desires that would go against what's "widely accepted" or imposed as "normal." For those of us who are bi- or pansexual, we often grow up performing heteroness because that's what we're culturally conditioned to believe we are.

Many couples choose to open up their relationship in order for one or both partners to explore sexual experiences with other genders. Beginning to pull on this thread can wind up unraveling more stuff related to compulsory monogamy.

Many couples choose to open up their relationship because there's something they want outside of their existing relationship. Beginning to pull on this thread can wind up unraveling more stuff related to compulsory heterosexuality.

So when we decide, "Hey, I want to explore non-monogamy," we're not just opening ourselves to more sex and different sexual situations. We're actually confronting some of the deepest patterns, assumed values, and carefully crafted identities that we've shaped from within our social contexts. When we are in the early stages of doing this kind of dismantling, rage, grief, upset, overwhelm, shutdown, etc. are all completely normal responses. Questioning these core components of who we are and how we learned to relate to the world around us can be scary, especially if we don't have a new operating system fully in place yet. Humans hate being in limbo. And I'm guessing if you're reading this book for personal purposes, you're one of the humans in this particular limbo of exploring non-monogamy in a dominantly monogamous heterosexual society. You are surprised at the level of discomfort you're experiencing, and you want some answers. I got you. I've been you.

2

FROM POST-TRAUMATIC PAIN
TO POLYAMOROUS PLEASURE

"Curiously enough, if we primarily try to shield ourselves from discomfort, we suffer. Yet when we don't close off and we let our hearts break, we discover our kinship with all beings."

— JANINA FISHER

Cozy, gentle, late-November light filled the Van Nuys guestroom where I was lying on the bed, naked and pondering. My week-long sexcapade with Itai was coming to an end, and I was trying to find my way to a different truth. I'd been seeing Itai sort of long-distance since the summer, the whole time telling anyone who would listen that there was no way it could turn into a serious thing. I was just having great sex with a hot guy who invited me to do things like hop on a plane with him to California for the week of Thanksgiving because he had a DJ gig in the desert and wanted some company. Faced with the prospect of a lonely turkey day in a new city where I had exactly one friend (who would be out of town), his invitation felt like just what I needed. The thing was, I hadn't expected to actually connect with him so much. I was actually afraid I was going to miss him when I boarded the plane back to Baltimore.

Because he was a traveling musician, his sex life had already been a topic amongst my friends; everyone was pretty decided he was getting laid all over the world. And, I mean, duh. The month before, he texted me from a gig in Mexico. He was down there playing for a lingerie fashion show. As I let my mind meander, I began to imagine him hooking up with other women. I imagined the sex, but I also imagined the moments bookending the sex ... the moments like the ones that he and I were having that summoned a different flavor of affection. Curiosity began to snowball around his other relationships. Suddenly I was both turned on and wanting to know about how he related to other romances. Getting to hear about a lover's adoration for women who I saw in a different light suddenly felt super attractive.

I think maybe I want an open relationship with this guy, I thought to myself.

On the drive to the airport, he looked over at me and said, "So, do we need to talk about this? Us?" My response prompted some pleasant surprise in him, and into the deep end we dove....

Neither of us had real experience in non-monogamy, outside of casually dating multiple people at once (or, you know, what some people just call dating). And I didn't even really have that; I had been mostly a serial monogamist with some drunken hookups sprinkled in between serious relationships since I was fifteen. Once I felt connected to someone, I felt completely attached to them. If there wasn't anyone I felt completely attached to, I had no idea how to authentically engage sexually or romantically. Consequently, I would get drunk to get laid. I considered myself sexually liberated because I knew how to almost always reach orgasm, and I didn't judge myself for these drunken shenanigans – that would be anti-feminist.

My last relationship spanned on-and-off most of my twenties, with me starring in the role of a co-dependent pretend-housewife to a rich husband whom I desperately wanted to save from his addictions in order to prove my worthiness, meanwhile distracting myself from my own pain and stunting my own healing. So, hearing that Itai had been single for several years because nobody had been as open to an open relationship scratched some kind of ego itch for me. (Of course, I would be the one to break the streak.)

When we first started, things were hot and heavy. It was super sexy hearing about his other dates. I genuinely felt happy for the other lovers getting to experience this wonderful human. My first threesome was a whole sexual revolution unto itself.

As we grew closer and became more attached, I struggled to find my own satisfaction in seeing other people. Since I had never really *dated* dated before, I was going through some of the normal, uncomfortable growing pains of learning how to navigate first dates. But on top of that, I was feeling isolated and lonely trying to jumpstart a new career in a city where I only had one friend. As my sense of loneliness grew, and in keeping with my romantic pattern, my relationship with Itai became the center of anything that felt good. And, as this sense of reliance grew, so did feelings of discomfort when he was with other people.

Despite the fact that I had fantasized about him with other women and had wanted to hear about what his other attractions were like, actually hearing about such things was making me feel inferior. What was wrong with me that I couldn't find people to date? It felt so unfair that he could just go play a gig and boom … a new lover would appear. As I watched him navigate his way through the world, I was simultaneously inspired and completely overwhelmed by envy. I yearned deep down in my bones to care less and have fun more.

At first, listening to his stories after dates had been exhilarating and sexy. It was a totally new type of bond to hear someone talk openly about how much fun they had with someone else, but that I was still present for them somehow. It felt like it reinforced the special thing that was uniquely ours that he would leave a date and immediately want to call to talk to me. But as our relationship deepened, it became less sexy and more triggering for me. Really, it became not sexy at all and only triggering for me. But wasn't this what I signed on for? Being jealous was something that came with the territory, and I was teaching myself to manage. *I shouldn't ruin the good time he's having,* I thought. *I'm just in a totally different place in life than he is and it's hard growing attached while being apart. It's not about the open relationship part.*

One night while he was halfway across the globe, I accepted an invitation to dinner with someone he had introduced me to, and his girlfriend. In all our speculative conversations leading up to the meeting, I thought my partner was saying, "I'd rather you didn't get sexually involved with this person in my life, but if you do, we will figure it out," and he thought he was saying, "I'm telling you it will be a problem for me if you do that." So, of course, when I did find myself in an intensely charged, kinky threesome and my first impulse was to call him and tell him what a crazy night I had, it did not go well.

Aside from being triggered himself, my partner was shocked that I was operating in a way that didn't consider his feelings. *Wait, what?* If you haven't yet dabbled in non-monogamy, that might sound a little loopy. Isn't part of the deal that you can sleep with other people – your partner might have feelings, but that's just part of it? Sort of…. If you have already dabbled in non-monogamy, you probably resonate with that feeling coming online, regardless of whatever agreements you've made.

The following weeks and months turned into a very confused version of my own personal hell; sleepless nights, long emotional conversations that left us totally depleted without making progress, and continued distress trying to get on the same page as my partner in our experience of non-monogamy. I felt almost rageful at what seemed like endless options for him when I would lose hours at a time on dating apps, with only creepy messages from married men to show for it. When he was away and with someone else, I would completely fall apart, doing whatever I could to stop myself from obsessively imagining what they were doing together.

Reprieve would come when he was finally alone again and could provide me the reassurance that he loved me, that he didn't want it to hurt like this for me. Calm and happiness would wash over my body momentarily, mimicking almost exactly the adrenaline high and then oxytocin flood of an abusive relationship cycle. Except that this wasn't abuse; he wasn't manipulating me. I was consenting to everything going on, telling myself that with time I would get better at managing the triggers. My understanding of trauma healing at that point was, "You heal by getting triggered and then writing a new ending to whatever that narrative was." For example, if my abandonment wound from my mother's death was being triggered every time my partner left, then these were all opportunities to re-write the narrative that says I end up abandoned. If I could just go through it enough times, I would learn. He would see.

After that major rupture, he came to Baltimore so we could do some repairing in person. We had both tried to lean on others for support and had come up empty-handed. The general response from our monogamous milieu was: "Well, it's an open relationship, what do you expect?" Not only was he hurt by my actions, but shocked to realize how unfulfilled I had been, when his experience of our relationship was only elevating the rest of his life. My "cool, chill girl" performance had fooled him. Watching him express this shock, I thought about the time he face-timed me from a gig so I would feel included in the dancing; he thought I was having fun with the music, but I had gone offscreen to cry.

I rapidly descended into the well that is toxic shame. I ran myself in circles trying to appease his anger and hurt. The way I knew to salvage relationships was to take as much responsibility as possible. So, of course, my answer here was to immediately jump to the narrative that I had "acted out" to get his attention. Yes, that was on me, and I was so sorry I didn't know how to communicate sooner. Couldn't he then see that I was just in pain and needed him and wouldn't he stay and prove that his love for me was more important than anything else in his life at that moment? Of course not, because he had better boundaries than I did at that point.

When he left for his next gig, I stayed awake at night crying hysterically. I regressed into the inconsolable girl whose mother was dying, who could do nothing to prevent the impending loss. All I wanted at that moment was to find a sense of security, and my body wouldn't allow me to do anything else but look for it.

After that next gig, he called me to say that nothing

sexual happened with anybody because he couldn't shake the feeling of how it would impact me. I was simultaneously relieved, grateful, and also now shame spiraling in a different direction. I got the reassurance of my importance but doing so had hurt the very person I wanted it from and hindered the kind of relationship structure I really wanted. I didn't consciously want to be controlling his actions or limiting his life, and I knew he was not happy with the impact I was having. We resolved to keep working on this, but I couldn't shake the feeling that I had been found out as the damaged one.

Sure enough, a few weeks later I had a full-blown meltdown. I had been diagnosed with complex-PTSD when I was younger, and with it came a Xanax prescription for when I would wake up in the middle of the night panicking. At the time, nobody told me that c-PTSD also means toxic shame, emotional flashbacks, ongoing sleep issues, and major challenges maintaining relationships. Since I came to Baltimore, I'd been slowly becoming more and more of an insomniac. I was increasingly emotionally volatile, and one day I finally snapped. My body was finally tired of its signals not being heeded, so it became inconsolable; I simply couldn't stop crying. And I don't just mean a trickle of tears feeling sad throughout the day. I mean violent sobbing with full body heaving that seemed to last forever. I face-timed a friend. I face-timed Itai. I didn't know what to do with myself, so consumed with raw, overwhelming emotion.

This episode was the rallying cry to finally face what needed healing around my pleasure. Conversations about what wasn't working for me, and my debilitating envy began to show me how I had deprioritized myself over the years, seemingly marching to the beat of my own drum, but internally desperately seeking approval. For the first time, maybe ever, I was seeing that *not* asserting my own wants created pain for someone I cared about. Forever the A- student (intensely devoted to learning the material, but time-blindness resulting in sloppy assignments), I committed myself to figuring this out.

The master's degree I had recently completed had given me a depth of knowledge how stress and trauma operate, and how to work with their impact. My training and prior experience as a clinical sexual health counselor had afforded me education, skills, and practice communicating frankly about sex. Surely, I could find ways to deepen and apply my knowledge of the body to what I was experiencing in this sexual and relational awakening. So, in addition to moving back to New England and getting back in therapy, I began my personal polyamorous education and pleasure renaissance. I needed to know what I truly desired beyond being desirable. I needed to figure out what I wanted aside from approval and accolades.

I'd been doing my own healing work for years already, but I hadn't yet confronted the parts that related to sexuality or polyamory. My complex-PTSD was the outcome of the shock waves sent through a family when a mother dies of cancer in her forties, leaving two children and their father absolutely bewildered. I'd been engaged in some combination of modalities for self-work since I was about nine, which had me on the archetypal path of the wounded healer. The summer Itai and I met, I was finishing a master's program in yoga therapy and was at the very beginning of establishing my private coaching practice. But how was it that throughout all of my training on healing and all of my education on sexuality (I was a trained sexual health counselor and doula), non-monogamy was something I didn't really have references for?

I said I got back in therapy, but the first therapist I saw in that period had zero experience with non-monogamy. Her favorite question was, "How might this be different if you were monogamous?" That relationship didn't last very long. I went through two more individual therapists (who both lasted longer, but were ill-equipped in other ways), several couples' therapists and coaches, and tons of wasted resources before finding someone who could give my polyamorous identity the space and support it needed. The struggle to find professional help that was actually helpful started my wheels spinning; if I was having this much trouble, certainly others were also in need. I made a promise to myself that if I could find my way to a more stable practice of non-monogamy, I'd pay it forward somehow.

Honestly, Itai and I made so many mistakes in the first couple of years because we had no guide, we had no community, we had no role models. When you're winging it, you will hurt each other. This isn't meant to shame or blame anyone, but just to acknowledge that we live in a world that makes this process hard. Patience and repair are essential. A few years later, polyamorous educator and coach Jessica Daylover asked me if we started our relationship as an open one. I told her not only that, but neither of us had experience or community that got it. She said, "Oh honey, you did exactly what I tell everyone absolutely not to do." We created so many ruptures that it took us a couple years to fully repair. But in those years, holy fuck what a transformation.

I read what I could get my hands on (which, at the time, was far less than is now available), hired a pleasure coach, took another more polyamorous and kink-positive sexuality training, and really, approached my own life as a case study for how to heal developmental trauma presenting in a non-monogamous life. I was repeatedly confronted with awareness that I couldn't advocate for what I wanted in the moment because I was hardly ever connected to what I wanted in the moment. Despite my vast education in both sex and embodiment, and the fact that I was building up a clientele of somatic coaching clients who were experiencing wonderful results, I was not nearly as grounded in my own body as I was outwardly presenting.

Slowly but surely, centering my own pleasure began to change everything, and not in the hedonistic way you might imagine. Centering my pleasure helped me step into parts of my sexuality that were yet unclaimed, shrouded in shame I didn't even know I had (three decades had passed by without me identifying my own queerness). The extra cool thing about claiming your sexual power is that the process of doing so transforms your relationship to your own desire, as well as your communication and boundaries – all the things essential to practicing non-monogamy. Focusing on feeling pleasure began to bring me back to my body. It taught me about my own worthiness. Expanding into a fuller sense of pleasure allowed me to grieve and release relationships from earlier chapters of my life that had disappointed me and left me alone. It helped me align to the values I hold most dear and ensure that I was actually embodying them.

As I healed these parts of me and re-claimed my pleasure, I began to see more clearly where my clients were also missing the benefits of pleasure in their daily lives. Every somatic coaching client I had seemed viscerally relieved when they realized they could talk to me about sex. I found it both fascinating and alarming that most of them would say, "I can't talk to my therapist about this," but that also reflected my experience. Few of them could provide details in response to "What do you really want?"

What they could identify more clearly was what they didn't want.

My work, much like my life, became more focused on fulfilling our birthright of pleasure. I created group programs to heal our cultural wounds around understanding and acting on our own desires, reprogramming the beliefs that they're selfish or that pursuing what we want hurts others. In collaboration with Itai, I began facilitating sex-positive events and nurturing the community that grew out of them. My one-on-one work with clients began to hone in on the experience of opening up to non-monogamy.

One day I found myself marveling at a life I hadn't previously even dreamed of; I was nurturing several different kinds of connections in my polyamory, having actual, liberated, fully-in-the-present-moment fun, and feeling supported and celebrated by the relationships showing up in my life. In recognition of the service our own healing can provide, my friend Rachael said to me, "You've got to write a book. This polyamorous party girl is an archetype we need." She's right, I thought. It's time for me to make good on my promise to pay it forward.

So here we are, dear poly-curious reader. What you have before you is the conglomerate wisdom from my decades of healing work, my own transition into non-monogamy and harnessing pleasure for trauma resolution, and how I've seen this body of knowledge apply to others. If you picked up this book, I'm guessing you're hurting, just as I was. I promise you, there is a path to pleasure.

3

RESOURCING YOUR EXPERIMENTATION

"When we liberate ourselves from the expectation that we must have all things figured out, we enter a sanctuary of empathy."

— SONYA RENEE TAYLOR

Firstand foremost, this is all an experiment. How we live and how we love are evolutions full of trial and error. This book is a resource to support your experimentation.

Before you dive in, I'd like to offer you some permission for your experimentation:

- Permission to go slow: urgency is counterproductive to healing. We integrate new information and intentionally change much better when we go slowly;
- Permission to take breaks: hyper-focusing on "fixing" a problem as complicated as this doesn't help you feel better. Especially if you notice your

body getting tense or alarms going off, take some time and space to do other things;

- Permission to fuck up: maintain your humanity by making mistakes. You're not supposed to do everything perfectly;
- Permission to trust yourself: only you are the expert on your life and your context. Everything offered here is intended to strengthen your own knowing of yourself. Make this material your own in whatever way makes sense to you.

For me, polyamory is both a spiritual practice and a healing practice. In both my understanding and experience, neither of those things have a linear path. We get lost or we get triggered, and we find our way back. And then it happens again, somewhere down the road. And again, and again, to varying degrees that we can't always predict. To me, the teachings of spirituality are about surrender. The path of healing, on the other hand, is about agency and choice. Our wounds develop from the moments in life when we've been disconnected from choice. Healing is about recovering our sense of agency. What's in this book is intended to help you clarify what you want and be better equipped to choose it.

Now, this book has lots of suggestions, exercises, and tools collected over many years, shaped by both evidence-based practice and personal experience. I do not advise implementing all of it at once – nobody can integrate that much so quickly.

If this book appeals to you, there's a very good chance you're currently in some emotional distress. The last thing emotional distress needs is pressure. Resist the urge to use this book to self-impose pressure. In fact, you might experiment with skimming through the whole thing once before you try any of the exercises.

I do recommend going in order, at least once through. The chapters do build off of each other, and you'll find some of the exercises make more sense having read the previous chapters. But you might be looking at the table of contents knowing already which chapter is most relevant to where you're at, and I'm not going to stop you from following your resonance.

This book is meant to be something you return to. Figuring out your right-fit non-monogamy is not like flipping a switch or stumbling upon the single a-ha moment that clicks everything into place. Like every long-term relationship, your relationship to how you relate is an evolution (meta enough for you?). The information, anecdotes, and exercises here will land differently at different moments in that evolution. So yes, you can work your way through all of it at this juncture and have that be greatly beneficial in stabilizing your overwhelm and enhancing your communication. But also know you can come back the next time something in your relational plane feels like too much and then have totally different discoveries.

One of the most beautiful things about non-monogamy is it challenges us to lean into uniqueness and difference. Every single relationship is different from other relationships and is full of differences within the connection itself. I prefer to mostly use the umbrella term "non-monogamy" because it leaves more space to ask for specificity. I find people generally have more pre-created meaning for terms like "polyamory," when in fact, "polyamory" can also mean many things. That said, these kinds of terms are necessary for conveying meaning, so it helps to have a general idea of what our shared meaning is. Below are some definitions for different relationship structure that may be relevant to you and your exploration. It is neither an absolute authority nor a complete glossary. If you are looking for more information, there is a key terms list in Jessica and Joseph Daylover's book, *Polyamory and Parenthood*, that I highly recommend.

I encourage everyone to consider what language truly feels like a right fit for self-identification, and also to always ask what people mean when they use a term from this or any other non-monogamy glossary. Most of these terms below reference sexual and romantic dynamics, but not everyone defines them that way. People on the asexual spectrum have just as much use for these terms as hyper-sexual folks. We all infuse our own meanings, and asking about someone's can be a wonderful way to not only find out if you're on the same page, but also invite intimacy.

NON-MONOGAMY GLOSSARY

Monogamy – two-person partnership with romantic and sexual exclusivity.

Monogamish – two-person partnership with some wiggle room. Usually when people say this, they are refer-ring to engaging with others sexually *together*, or having some specific scenarios in which it's OK to sexually engage outside of the two-person partnership (things like "hall passes," one-night-stand-only situations, or if one partner has sexual desires that don't align with the monogamous relationship they can specifically seek out the fulfillment of those dynamics but not others).

Open relationship – typically, a two-person relationship in which both humans are welcome to engage in connec-tions with others outside of the two-person dynamic. This can take a wide variety of forms, but generally that means sexual or romantic engagements. For some, the door is open to develop other long-term dynamics, and for others, an open relationship means specifically short-term.

Polyamory – relationships where sexually and / or romantically engaging with others is an option. Being polyamorous can refer to both identity and relational structure; you might be polyamorous but not currently in any relationship, and that doesn't detract from the identity of polyamorous. Some people identify as polyamory and include intimate platonic partnerships in their definition of this love style.

- Triad: when three people are involved with each other in an ongoing and committed manner (can be open or closed). Arguably the most challenging structure to intentionally seek out, especially without prior experience in non-monogamy. Different from a threesome, which typically refers to a sexual encounter between three people.
- Kitchen-table polyamory: when partners of partners know and engage with each other.
- Solo poly: when a person is open to engage with multiple romantic and / or sexual relationships, while prioritizing their relationship with self (technically this is ideal no matter what structure you follow). Solo poly people often (but not always) are more explicit about not having a desire to "escalate" relationships in accordance with our cultural defaults. More likely to not live with sexual or romantic partners in order for logistics to more easily support the ideology.
- Parallel: when multiple relationships are consensual, but partners of partners do not meet or engage with each other.

- QPP: "queer platonic partner" is a partnership that does not primarily include sexual or romantic engagement but plays a partnership role in someone's life.

Metamour: a partner's partner.

Compersion: the pleasure we feel as a result of a partner experiencing pleasure (when it doesn't directly involve us).

Hierarchical relationships: when one relationship is prioritized over others. If you are opening an existing relationship and have agreed that that relationship comes first, that is a hierarchical dynamic.

Relationship anarchy: the counterpoint to hierarchical relationships.

Relationship escalator: the societally prescribed progression of an intimate partnership – i.e., dating, moving in together, getting married, having kids.

Couple's privilege: the privilege afforded to couples by society. Shows up in other relationship dynamics and particularly in hierarchical structures, can negatively impact other partners by unconsciously prioritizing the established / married / "more serious" couple.

Now that you can navigate the basic non-monogamy vernacular, let's begin with this – what do you think you want out of non-monogamy? Why? What types of experiences would you like to have? Why? What role would you like your existing partner to play in that? Why?

Do you have a sense of wanting this long-term, i.e., is there a bigger vision for you? Or is this more like a curiosity you want to follow or an experiment you want to try on?

Are you crystal clear on the answers? Or do you feel perplexed? Maybe overwhelmed?

If you feel clear on your answers, but hazy on how to get there, you'll probably benefit most from focusing your energy on the exercises provided. (And, a friendly reminder that clarity is useful for identifying desire, but as we learn more and experience new things, desire does change.)

For those feeling more perplexed, and maybe like you bit off more than you can chew, I invite you to notice your internal experience as you read the concepts in this book. This book may act as a brainstorm for you. See how your body responds to the ideas presented, and then return to the questions above once you have more of a sense of what's entailed.

This book is going to help you understand first how to recognize what's going on in your own experience and your own body because transitioning to non-monogamy is a complicated process and you can't just think your way through it; we've got to get your body and your mind working together. Your body and your holistic sense of pleasure will then be your guides as we explore what makes existing relationships unique and magical without relying on the structure of monogamy. We will tap into the importance of prioritizing your pleasure and the necessary skills for doing so (especially if you come from people-pleasing and perfectionism). The later chapters will dive into how to communicate, how to navigate conflict, and what collaboration in *your* non-monogamy means.

Who this book is FOR:

- Those who have begun opening up and are experiencing a new level of anxiety, moodiness, despair, or overwhelm as a direct result;
- Anyone feeling confused or frustrated by how much they desire a non-monogamous lifestyle but how hard it is in practice;
- Couples who are opening their relationship and experiencing an increase in conflict;
- Folks who are considering changing their current relationship structure or approach to intimacy;
- Monogamous friends and family who want to learn more about the experience of non-monogamous people in their life;
- Anyone interested in learning skills for deeper connection and more aligned relationships (whether non-monogamous or not!).

What this book is NOT:

- A replacement for psychotherapy, medical care, or actual coaching;
- Going to help you if you are in an abusive, narcissistic, or coercive dynamic;
- A solution. Because there isn't one. You are a complex, messy human, and so are all the people in your life. We're not trying to "fix" that, we're

aiming to empower you to navigate that as your happiest self.

- Doing the work of your partner.
- A comprehensive guide with an all-encompassing perspective. There is much to learn about non-monogamy beyond the scope of these pages, and from perspectives very different than mine. Check out the back of the book for some other recommendations.

If you are reading this looking for answers about how to change your partner's behavior, pause. First, you can't change their behavior. If their behavior is harming you or putting you at risk and they don't express interest in accountability (or at least better understanding your experience), I implore you to either break up or seek counseling with a trained professional. Second, if they are not also putting in their fair share of the labor trying to understand and do better, ask yourself if you want to be in a relationship that doesn't prioritize equity, *and why*.

Now then, time to set up a cozy reading space, grab a favorite beverage, and anything else that invites you to have an enjoyable experience while exploring your inner landscape. Most of the chapters ahead have prompts and exercises to help you apply the concepts to your own life, so it's a good idea to have something to write with, And of course, may pleasure be your guide.

4

CENTERING THE BODY TO
SUPPORT THE MIND

*"You've dealt with the stressor," I said, "but not the stress. Your
bodies still think you're being chased by the lion."*

— EMILY NAGOSKI

I f you've made it this far in the book, I'm guessing
you've experienced some pretty dramatic responses
to situations you've encountered through non-
monogamy. Before we dive into any how-to or advice-type
stuff, let's first make sure we're on the same page about
what's *actually* happening. What you absolutely must
understand for anything else in this book to be useful to
you is that emotions are signals that come from the body.
Our feelings of love, connection, joy, curiosity, trust, intimacy are all different expressions of the electrical signals
that come through us when our body assesses that it is safe
(or not reacting to a perceived threat). When we feel rage,
overwhelm, anxiety, numbness, upset – those are emotions
born of the body assessing that it is unsafe somehow –

either a violation of some kind has occurred, or it needs to be on alert for something that will threaten its safety.

Learning the language of our own body helps us better understand how to create safety for it. It's bodily safety that will make the difference between white-knuckling your way through constant anxiety and finding consistent enjoyment in your non-monogamy.

WINDOW OF TOLERANCE / SOCIAL ENGAGEMENT THROUGH THE BODY

Have you ever had a complete meltdown in front of someone else and heard them tell you to "calm down"? In the entire history of big human emotions, do you think that "advice" has ever worked? Probably not. Why? Because those big emotions are expressions of a nervous system saying, "I'm not safe." To calm ourselves down requires the same nervous system to suddenly respond to the unchanged context by saying, "Oh, actually, never mind. This is safe." The mind that's saying, "Calm down," and the body saying, "I'm not safe," are not speaking the same language. To make use of this book, we have to tell your body to calm down, but in its own language. So, here's an abridged version of the language your body speaks.

Your central nervous system's number-one job is to keep you safe and alive. It does this by interpreting cues from your environment as well as signals from inside your body and making an assessment: safe or unsafe. Based on that assessment, it sends signals back to the body to regulate your heart rate, temperature, digestion, pretty much every bodily function.

When the body assesses itself as generally safe, we call this being in the window of tolerance. In this window, our body experience has a range of physiological states that are considered healthy, for the most part. Our heart rate, blood pressure, metabolism, concentration, problem-solving, etc. are all operating at a baseline that can deviate to respond to stressors, but stays within a certain range. When we are in our window of tolerance, we are able to engage the aspects of our physiology that create connection and intimacy with other people. This often includes things like listening, steady and calm tone of voice, eye contact, pleasurable physical contact. We call this function of our nervous system our "social engagement system" because it gives us access to emotions like empathy, curiosity, and compassion. When we are in our window of tolerance, we have more access to our social engagement system, as well as the part of our brain most responsible for complex thought and problem-solving. This makes us more capable of self-regulation, meaning that we have more command over how we interact with our emotions; they are one part of the show, but we are capable of managing them as opposed to them managing us.

When we find ourselves outside of the window of tolerance, our body is either having a hyper- or a hypo-response to an assessment of "unsafe." Hyper-responses are those that activate us: get us all amped up to either go to battle with our perceived threat or run like hell in the opposite direction. They increase our heart rate so our muscles can get more oxygen, they increase our focus and alertness, etc.; you've likely heard the saber tooth tiger story before. Hypo-responses shut us down; in their more extreme versions essentially saying, "You don't stand a chance of defeating this threat, so go ahead and play dead." This can look like cooling down the body to conserve energy, not being able to verbally communicate, feeling sluggish in the body and foggy in the mind, numbness, or disassociation. If you've ever experienced overwhelming shame, you might recall the feeling of wanting to curl up in a little ball and not be seen. That is hypo-arousal.

Now, these hyper- and hypo-responses don't always necessarily take us outside our window of tolerance. Depending on our capacity to digest the signals of the body and the resources we have for resilience, we may be within the range of that window, and then these responses are simply in the realm of stress. When we are in the realm of digestible stress, we are still able to access listening, empathy, communication, etc. When we are experiencing stress, but in the window of tolerance, we can take in other information that may change how we interpret the threat.

For example, you're standing outside the movie theater waiting for your partner, who is late and hasn't reached out, which is very unlike them. You're starting to cross the threshold from annoyed to a little anxious, scanning the parking lot for signs of his car arriving, compulsively checking your phone to see if they called back, pacing and fidgeting, squeezing yourself with your arms crossed over your chest. When they arrive, they apologize and explain that their phone completely broke as they were driving. Obviously, they couldn't call, and they were late because they didn't know the way without GPS. They give you a big hug as they apologize for the impact this has on you, and your body receives the combination of physical touch, the explanation, and their attunement to your experience as signals that change your assessment of potential danger – your body registers "safety" once again. What was starting to feel unsafe has been resolved, and you can go into the movie calm, albeit a little disappointed about missing the previews.

In this example, another human helps us return to that sense of safety. Similarly, this is how our nervous systems first develop and learn to distinguish "safe" from "unsafe." What I mean by that is that humans are social creatures, not just in the fact that we like to socialize and connect, but that when we are born, we are a species of some of the most helpless, vulnerable newborns. Some animals come into this life with bodies capable of meeting their own needs for survival, but humans are not one of them. We are wired to cry out when we are hungry, to communicate with some other human who can tend to that need for us. There is a very, very deep knowing in our bodies that our survival depends upon those with whom we form attachments. So further down the road, when you have formed an attachment to a partner and then your body perceives that attachment as threatened somehow, the logical interpretation in your body's language might be that your very survival is being threatened.

Our ability to metabolize stress depends on many factors, like what coping mechanisms we've developed, how life experiences have conditioned us, and also things as basic as how much rest and food we've gotten. One of the things that can impact this capacity for resilience is just how much stress load we're dealing with. That can mean having multiple different stressors at once – think chronic stress of living, working, raising kids in late-stage capitalism without health insurance. Or stressors of a different caliber – think violent attack or sudden loss. When our resilience is lessened (as it is with chronic stress) and / or we perceive truly scary, harmful, or violent things, these stress responses turn into something bigger and the body becomes primarily focused on whatever it *thinks* is necessary to resolve the threat and return to safety.

Let's revisit that movie theater scenario for a moment, but this time you're under pressure at work, you've been having trouble sleeping, and your beloved aunt who basically raised you is in the hospital. Your system is under-resourced, or rather, the fuel you need is spread too thin. So when your partner is running late and you can't reach them, the impact is greater. By the time they arrive, you've started imagining terrible things or cursing them in your head, and when they reach out to hug you, you pull away from their touch. You go inside to the movie, but the whole time your thoughts are still focused on what could have happened, how inconsiderate your partner was to you, and how they should really take better care of their things or have back-up plans for situations like this. You sit with your arms crossed, and the muscles in your face are tense as you try to act like you're focused on the movie. This is a version of your system focusing on what it perceives as a threat even after the actual moment of threat has passed (when you didn't know where your partner was or if they were OK). Your system recognizes that the threat of your partner disappearing is no longer real, but it has not re-established the perception of safety, so it continues to search for things that could still be a problem for you.

A similar experience often happens early in non-monogamy, for example, the first time a partner sleeps with someone else or spends the night with another partner. We might become fixated on imagining what they're doing, how they didn't keep the agreement we made about when to text goodnight, or even all the reasons why this relationship is actually not right and we should break up when they come back the next morning. If we have repeated experiences like this without digesting the physiological stress that they bring up, rather than getting more accustomed to these scenarios, they can actually become more triggering for us. Eventually, we find ourselves in unmanageable states of anxiety and overwhelm, signaling that we are actually outside the window of tolerance.

Outside the window of tolerance, it becomes much harder for us to communicate and connect with other human beings. These big responses that take us out of our window of tolerance are fight, flight, and freeze. Fight and flight are the hyper-responses and freeze is the hypo-response. When our body gets "stuck" in one of these responses outside of the window of tolerance, we refer to this as the impact of trauma. So, if you've ever heard things like, "Trauma lives in the body," or "The body keeps the score," that's part of what we mean.

Past trauma shows up in our relationships not just in the form of *what* our triggers are, but how the communication and conflict surrounding those triggers plays out. If you recall a really gnarly fight with a beloved partner, can you remember what it felt like in your body? Often hyper-arousal will come with shorter, shallower breath, jumpy thoughts, and increased irritability. And suddenly that activation in our body is acting out a memory from another time you felt that way, making it impossible to listen for what your partner is trying to say in the present because internally your body is shouting about something from the past.

FAWNING AS A SURVIVAL STRATEGY

Where humans get really complicated and interesting is in our fawn response (sometimes known as "befriend"). Most people have at least heard of the fight and flight responses because they've become somewhat ubiquitous with stress, and it's easier to recognize feeling those expressions of stress in the body. Fawning is a little more nuanced because it's not just a physiological response in the body, but a behavioral adaptation that results from being in conditions where the other responses aren't effective. The other thing we mean when we say humans are social beings is that the nervous system is designed to reach for supportive human connection as its first response to perceived threat. If that doesn't work, then it moves to hyper-arousal (which can include other forms of social connection). And if that doesn't work, then it moves to hypo-arousal. (This is just based on design, not contextual conditioning or epigenetics.) But because we rely so heavily on social relationships for our survival, we can sometimes prioritize maintaining connection to another person at all costs – this is the fawn response, and it can involve varying degrees of hyper- and hypo- depending on the person.

Fawning is when we set aside our own wants, desires, and individuated needs to appease and prioritize someone else's preferences, desires, and needs, because some part(s) of us interpret(s) that our connection to this person (and therefore our social safety, therefore our survival) will be threatened if we assert our difference. You can think of it as people-pleasing to avoid conflict and earn approval. In fact, it is essentially people-pleasing, but a more dramatic presentation because it became habitual in developmental years. Fawning is often not conscious, and frequently less readily identified than fight, flight, or freeze because it is primarily embodied by the absence of something, not a presence of other signals. Part of the unconscious conditioning comes from recognizing that their behaviors or submission are capable of calming down an agitated caregiver. When they see someone getting upset, fawning might be the body's attempt to co-regulate. This means fawning is primarily marked by the suppression of one's own desires and curiosities, an absence of what we do want in clear and specific terms, while contorting ourselves in varying degrees to fit others. It also means our body internalizes that other people's emotions are our responsibility to manage. If you are a people-pleaser, perfectionist, or peacemaker, there's a high likelihood you've engaged in fawning at some point. All of these are different expressions of the body understanding that safety comes from attachment that is conditional, relying upon our ability to make others happy, perform according to their standards, or keep our opinions to ourselves if they will challenge someone else's sense of harmony.

Some signs you might be fawning include having no sense of your authentic self, being *overly* helpful and concerned whether others will perceive you as helpful, always waiting for others to voice their opinion before you give yours, or hyper-awareness about what others think of you. If you are particularly conflict-averse or have a hard time receiving critical feedback, that may also point to fawning tendencies.

If our survival depends on others, then fawning is actually a pretty smart way to respond to feeling threatened, right? Yes, *and* it's just not sustainable for our bodies. Just like the other three trauma responses, fawning is meant to be a temporary survival strategy. While we are fawning, we are essentially disconnecting from our own internal cues to survive a situation of threat. We can't stay disconnected from our own internal cues for long periods without it taking a toll on us. When we are disconnected from our internal cues, it is impossible to be in a consensual relationship with ourselves. It's kind of like trying to navigate sexual consent when totally inebriated or seeking medical consent without explaining the procedure; the person can't give consent if they can't digest what they're consenting to. You can't operate consensually with yourself if you can't feel your own signals.

Our dominant culture feeds off of fawning, so many of

us don't realize we're doing it, or don't realize the full extent to which it's harming us. Non-monogamy will ask us to more directly confront how people-pleasing does not actually get our needs met.

If you are exploring non-monogamy primarily because your partner wanted to and you don't want to lose them, things likely won't go well. The same is true in specific scenarios *within* non-monogamy. It's OK to agree to explore even if you're on the fence, but we want to make sure that exploration is what *you* want from the scenario, not just making your partner happy.

I see this come up often in scenarios where it appears as though one partner is either asserting more expertise about non-monogamy or having an easier time navigating it. When we start this process, we don't know what we don't know, and many of us come to non-monogamy thinking, "If we're doing this, we're doing it." We dive in with very little understanding of what our own boundaries are and have read things to the tune of, "Your jealousy is yours to deal with." If your partner seems to be breezing through the transition, enjoying the dating process, and dismissing your feelings of fear and jealousy as "just part of the deal," while you feel overwhelmed and exhausted, there's a good chance fawning is at play.

My client Allie spent several months opening her relationship with her partner in a way that didn't work for her. Their discussions had reached the agreement that they could both date whomever they wanted, and develop both sexual and romantic bonds with other people. Allie was slowly watching her emotional reactions to her partner's dating grow in intensity, but she couldn't pinpoint why. It took some time, but eventually Allie told me, "I don't think I want us to be dating other people. I just want us to be exploring sex differently." That clarity of desire was something she had suppressed in order to go along with what her partner wanted.

Fawning can also be tricky in opening to new sexual situations, particularly for folx who were raised as women or femmes. One of the most publicly prevalent reasons for opening up is for a woman in a heterosexual couple to explore sexual attraction to other genders. In my own experience with this, it took several instances of pursuing women with my partner to realize I was *trying* to pursue my own desire, but in the moments of sexual contact, I was primarily going along with how sex worked for him. Whereas he had years of experience with women, I had essentially none. I was intimidated and needed to move slower in order to feel comfortable, but also didn't want to be seen as holding things back.

Of these four Fs (fight, flight, freeze, fawn), most of us have a default we go to more readily when our body perceives threat. This is born of a mixture of things, primarily your own physiology paired with your actual life experiences. Part of what happens for many of us who have relied on fawning in the past is that the new relational structure forces us to confront how fawning has shaped us; it brings us startlingly into contact with a dynamic in which fawning *really* won't work to establish safety. Suddenly our default survival mechanism is rendered void, and we lose any sense of competency in establishing our own felt sense of security. That seems like a pretty valid reason that we'd be stuck outside our window of tolerance, right?

Why is it so important to understand your window of tolerance in opening up your relationship? Because if we get too far outside of it too often, it actually will shrink. Then everything becomes more triggering, and non-monogamy may actually have the impact of traumatizing us. If we work to gradually expand our window of tolerance, we build more capacity more quickly and can move toward the relationships we want without every little thing feeling like a giant hurdle to overcome. In this case, non-monogamy actually has the potential to heal old traumas.

CALMING DOWN

So how do we navigate this? How do you help yourself back to the window of tolerance even as you throw your old relating scripts out entirely?

Well, I know nobody likes to hear this, but you've gotta calm down. According to the Gottman Institute, a leading relationship research center, "The more 'diffusely physiologically aroused' (in other words, in 'fight or flight' mode,) someone is during a conflict conversation, the more his or her marital satisfaction is likely to decline during a period of three years." (https://www.gottman.com/about/research/faq/).

And this may seem a little patronizing, but while you learn to speak the language of your body, think of it the same way as learning to speak any other language; you need Post-It notes all over your house. No, seriously. In the midst of your body's next big reaction, you will not remember whatever I'm about to tell you in the rest of this chapter. You will likely be so caught up yelling at your partner in your head or pacing back and forth or crying hysterically that your brain will need something outside of itself to actually implement these tools. (These survival mechanisms are very good at what they do, after all, and that is keeping us focused on the perceived threat.) So, find a way to structure your reminders. That could also be planning with a friend or creating daily practices … but more on that later.

For now, consider the regulation of the body "Calming Down 101."

Regulation

For our purposes, regulation means staying within or returning to the window of tolerance, so that we can engage our social connection system. Most often a regulated state means you can take deep breaths with ease, stay in the realm of embarrassment rather than shame, look at things from other perspectives, feel most of your body, express yourself, listen and take in new information, focus, and access creativity and compassion. Things like neurodivergence can impact what your specific markers of regulation are, but the bottom line is being able to connect, both with yourself and others.

When you start to notice yourself moving toward dysregulation (the Fs), we want to employ tools that will help you maintain regulation, or stay in your window of tolerance. That can either happen as co-regulation or self-regulation.

But before you dive deep trying to find the perfect tools, start with basics: have a glass of water, and maybe a snack and a nap. Most of the time if we're getting dysregulated, hydration, nourishment, and rest will help. At the very least, drinking water activates the nerve that facilitates your relaxation response and increases your odds of the following being effective.

Co-Regulation

This refers to what you do with another being (or multiple beings) to offset / manage the body's response to perceived threats and either stay within or return to the window of tolerance. (*Most often we think of this as two people, but it can also be nature or animals that co-regulate with you. In this book, we are speaking about it as a human-to-human practice.*) I personally feel our culture de-prioritizes co-regulation, so I like to emphasize it as an important skill to build. Yes, self-regulation is also important, but because our nervous systems reach for social engagement as the first response to threat, I think it's helpful for us to re-learn that natural design.

- Breathing together
- Engaging curiosity
- Physical touch
- Playfulness
- Dancing
- Taking a walk
- Talking and active listening (about anything other than what is activating you)
- Creating together
- Singing together

Self-Regulation

Self-regulation is what you do for yourself to offset / manage the body's response to perceived threats and either stay within or return to the window of tolerance. If you are particularly dysregulated in response to what's going on in relation to a partnership, it may not work for that partner to be a source of co-regulation. You may find it more useful to lean into self-regulating *before* trying to address the issue with them.

- Shaking your body (imitate a dog coming out of the rain until you feel a shift)

- Sounding (like OM-ing or humming, or just letting sound come out of your mouth)
- Intentional tantrum-ing (yelling into pillow or punching cushions)
- Journaling
- Exercise
- Somatic orienting
- Breathing
- Taking a walk
- Singing
- Taking a bath
- Self-massage

If you are experiencing major dysregulation (like panic or freeze responses), I encourage finding someone to work with who is both trauma-informed and polyam-competent. If that is not available to you, you may find some relief with the following:

- Ice pack on chest (for hyperarousal, not hypoarousal)
- Heating pad or something warming on low back
- Extra sleep / rest, however you need to get it
- Balancing (as simple as shifting weight to one foot or as complicated as your most advanced balancing yoga postures)

(If you want some help identifying the regulation tools and practices that are most supportive to you specifically, check out the link provided at the back of the book. I made you a class that comes with a worksheet.)

If we're used to either ignoring signals from the body or interpreting them through a different lens than their own language, it can take some time to make the changes that prioritize the window of tolerance. Hell, it can take us a while to even identify our window of tolerance. But I promise it's worth it. Now that you understand *why* we need to speak the language of the body, we'll discuss guidelines and tools that helps us do so in non-monogamy.

5

A TRAUMA-SENSITIVE APPROACH TO NON-MONOGAMY

"We are able to stand up for what we believe in and ask for what we need from a place of regulation rather than from a state of protection."

— DEB DANA

Trauma is essentially about connection, or rather, broken connection. It is not about the "what happened" but about the resulting impact in our body. The window of tolerance signifies a body-state in which we are able to connect. When we are outside our window of tolerance for too long, struggling to return to our physiological state for connection, this is considered trauma. Intense anxiety and overwhelm can be signs we're dealing with a trauma imprint, which is part of why it's important for us to acknowledge trauma when we're discussing how to approach non-monogamy.

In its very structure, non-monogamy has different risks for triggering trauma imprints than monogamy. As you consent to your partner having other kinds of relationships with other people, you potentially open yourself to feelings of rejection and / or abandonment. These are two of the human experiences that create trauma, particularly when we are younger. If you've been monogamous until now, you may have stabilized your relationship with these feelings enough to not have them impact your life very much. As you confront them more in non-monogamy, they may bring up memories in the body that stir up big reactions.

Now, I want to introduce you to some basic guidelines for trauma resolution, because if you can apply these to your practice of non-monogamy, you will almost certainly be moving at a pace and in a way that works better for you. Approaching non-monogamy through a lens of trauma resolution (as a couple or polycule) also minimizes the risk of having traumatizing (or re-traumatizing) experiences. On top of that, if we are looking to heal wounds that have been inflicted by past relationships or compulsory heteromonogamy, this is the way that gets to happen.

Rachael Maddox's ABCs of trauma resolution is a set of skills she teaches to coaches, therapists, healers, and other space-holders, completely separate from anything having to do with non-monogamy. But they are wonderful guideposts for navigating anything that has the potential to traumatize or re-traumatize us, and can be adapted beautifully to apply to your approach to non-monogamy. Implementing these principles builds a strong foundation for less overwhelm and anxiety in your non-monogamy experience.

ATTUNEMENT

Attunement can also be understood as being present, but with a little more specificity. Attunement means "tuning in" to the here and now, noticing what is true in the context of the present moment and physical space. Attunement is a requirement of intimacy, because without it we cannot see or hear each other.

When my partner is away or out, I am home alone scrolling Instagram on the couch, and my mind starts feeding me stories about how much fun he's having meeting people who are more aligned with him, and who will become more important to him than I am, there is a lack of attunement. I am not noticing the here, the now, or the truth. Instead, I am leaping to an imaginary future.

When my partner is full of new relationship energy and can't seem to put his phone down from texting his new partner while I am cooking us a meal or watching T.V. beside him, there is a lack of attunement. He is not noticing the here and now of my attempts at connecting with him, twisting in the knife of feeling forgotten, not cared for. (P.S.: This is part of why phones are massively detrimental to intimate relationships in general, not just if someone is texting another partner.)

Attunement looks like paying attention to each other, making observations about what you see, hear, and feel in your partner. Attunement looks like beginning conversations with "How are you?" and actually listening for the answer. Attunement feels like your partner is responsive to your expressions and state of being. Attunement in non-monogamy might look like being at a play party, noticing that someone in the interaction suddenly feels disconnected, and stopping what's happening to check in.

"Somatic listening" is a great practice for honing your

attunement skills. Rather than active listening, in which we are keenly paying attention to information, somatic listening is a practice in which we're also paying attention to sensation. This helps us with attunement because attunement is something that happens at a body level more than a cognitive level. I also recommend this practice because it helps us embody staying in our own experience, rather than abandoning ourselves to manage someone else's emotions. It helps us embody the boundary between their feelings and how I choose to respond to their feelings.

To practice somatic listening, sit face to face with a partner. Before either of you begins speaking, notice what your posture feels like, and take in a sense of their body. As your partner speaks, you remain quiet. Try to split your awareness fifty-fifty between receiving what they are communicating and tracking your own experience in your body; how is your breath, your temperature, any sensations? Our nervous systems are always communicating with each other more subtly than our cognitive minds are drawn to. This way of listening helps us notice more about what's being communicated non-verbally.

BODY-BASED

The body-based (or somatic) guideline has to do with your ability to sense your body's states and cues. This is a physiological mechanism called interoception and it is the foundation of emotional wellness. Our success in navigating the communication, conflict, and collaboration involved in relationships depends upon our ability to sense our *impulses, instincts, needs, and desires.*

Cues of temperature, pain, hunger, thirst, neutrality, expansion, contraction, comfort, pleasure, weightedness, speed, buoyancy, gravity, energy, fluidity, texture, and more can give us important signals about where we are in relation to the window of tolerance. As renowned trauma therapist Deb Dana says, "Story follows state." This means the state of the autonomic nervous system dictates the story we perceive about our current experience.

If we are in the window of tolerance, we are more able to attune and interpret a story based on the present moment. If we are in a hyper-response, we are more likely to experience narratives with an "emergency" tone, or a combative energy. When something is upsetting you and you find yourself rehearsing angry conversations in your head, that is likely related to a hyper-response. When you find yourself saying things like, "I don't know," "I don't care," or not having strong feelings about anything, that is more in line with hypo-responses.

As you can imagine, this matters in relationships, because the narrative lens through which we experience the relationship can either be detrimental or supportive. The Gottman Institute conducted a study on physiology in couples' conflicts and found that increased indicators of a fight or flight response were linked to decreasing marital satisfaction within three years. This makes sense if we consider that defensiveness is an expression of fight or flight. By definition, when we are defensive, we struggle to access empathy or compassion. The more fight or flight, the more defensiveness and, therefore, the less compassion, which is essential for intimacy.

In the process of opening up, we will likely get dysregulated to some degree. We are consciously building new understandings of our relationships, and it can take time for the body to catch up. So we want to center the body's cues, help it regulate, and prioritize amplifying the signals we associate with the window of tolerance, or our social engagement system. This means:

- listening to and honoring my impulses, instincts, needs, and desires;
- working on a consensual relationship with my own body as the foundation for how I show up in other relationships; beginning to notice when and why I suppress what my body is asking for;
- learning the cues that signal my dysregulation;
- learning to read the cues that my partner is dysregulated;
- respecting and appreciating when my partner does the same;
- reminding ourselves that the narrative mind is often an expression of the body's state – what happens to my panic about our relationship if I can calm the panic in my body?
- building up practices (solo and with partners) that support our regulation.

CONSENT AND COOPERATION

Consent is about building trust, respecting limits, and empowering choice. Ideally, consent is a collaborative process. By attuning to ourselves, and operating in a way that prioritizes our own body, we build self-consent, the foundation for how we show up in other relationships. When we have a baseline of operating consensually in how we treat ourselves (meaning not forcing ourselves to do things we don't like, or consistently going beyond our own limits with work, social obligations, etc.), how we participate in consent with others is more authentic.

In helping professions, "informed consent" refers to

ensuring the client has enough information to understand their options and the context for their decisions. In our relationships, we want to also apply this: Do you have the information you need to make an informed choice? Are you giving others the information that is relevant for them to exercise their agency? For example, if you're in an open relationship, is that something you inform new partners of? Is that information people need about you in order to make the right choice for them? Consent means centering agency in collaboration, while cooperating with whatever is showing up in the present moment.

By cooperation, we mean working *with* whatever signals are present, rather than trying to override them. Trusting the process of the body's inherent wisdom and blueprint of interconnectedness by allowing what is, working *with* what exists in the relational and physiological field rather than forcing things to be different or adhering to specific interventions. For example, it is a common misperception that if we've committed to a polyamorous relationship, anything goes, and that applies right away. If you are having an overwhelming response to something going on between your partner and one of their partners, and they tell you, "You shouldn't be so upset, sleeping with him was within our agreements. If this is going to work you need to stop making me feel so guilty about doing what you said was OK," that is not cooperating.

Instead, cooperation might sound like, "Wow, I see this is a bigger response than either of us were expecting. Does it need anything from us right now? Is there a response to this big reaction that would feel supportive?"

DOABILITY & TITRATION

Remember when I said previously that getting out of your window of tolerance repeatedly and / or for long periods of time can have the effect of actually decreasing the window itself? That's because human physiology prefers to stay the same: this is called homeostasis. Our nervous system dictates the rate at which we can incorporate change, whether or not we like it; if we try to push for change faster than the nervous system can integrate, it will find a way to balance itself out. It is actually a more efficient approach to our growth to stay in the realm of doability, in alignment with the present moment desires and instincts. (Bonus tip: If you're trying to override your present moment desires, you are not in consent with yourself, which will also cause problems.)

Titration is how we dose doability. Technically, titration is mixing two substances to achieve a desired alchemy. Then pausing and seeing how they integrate. Titration is a method that makes sure we are careful not to cause explosions, and also asks us to find the edge of transformation. When a window of tolerance has decreased, titration is one of the ways we build it back up.

Now this is the one that becomes a little bit tricky in non-monogamy, usually because it means going slower than we want to, titrating new experiences with other partners, new situations that might be challenging, etc. It is also good to be aware that it is likely to impact outside partners in a way that inherently prioritizes the couple. Be sure you're communicating with all parties involved, but I know that doesn't tend to happen when people are embarrassed that they're not "better" at this, or their philosophy is taking priority over their body.

For example, Noel did a lot of research before opening

his relationship. He read all the books, blogs, and educational social media he could find, and felt very strongly about not exercising what is referred to in polyamory as "couples' privilege." This means he didn't want the existing relationship to interfere with the other relationships his partner was building. But as Noel's partner, Kat, was deepening intimacy rather quickly with two other people, Noel started having anxiety attacks. When I asked Noel how Kat was interacting with this, he told me, "I don't want to tell her because it feels like failing at doing something I really believe in. I'm afraid to be the reason she pulls back from other relationships." Sometimes, I explained to Noel, we need something we deem "less ideal" at first in order to get to the point of embodying what we do believe in.

Noel and Kat decided to try a version of titrating in which they committed to a date together in between each date apart. Kat's other partners agreed that they ultimately wanted Noel to feel OK in his body for the sake of the overall dynamic, so they were understanding about moving slower for some time. This support from relative strangers helped Noel's body feel much more trusting of their presence in his life, and the dates with Kat in between her other dates gave Noel more clarity about what he needed to feel secure. The anxiety attacks disappeared.

Titration of challenging experiences can be very, very useful in the doability of opening up. First because it doesn't overwhelm our system. Second because it also teaches us a ton about what is supportive for us in coming back together, in integrating effectively. It structures enough time for us to learn about our integration process, rather than bounce from one experience to another without understanding what we need in order to feel more supported and connected.

YOUR ABCS:

With your notepad and paper, jot down either an example of how you are currently implementing it or a possible way you could apply it to your relationship(s) for each of the ABCs: Attunement, Body-Based, Consent & Cooperation, and Doability & Titration.

Bonus points if you and your partner share your lists with each other.

6

THE POWER OF PLEASURE

"Pleasure is the point. Feeling good is not frivolous, it is freedom."

— ADRIENNE MAREE BROWN

P eople have all different kinds of reasons for exploring non-monogamy, each of them just as valid as another (I really mean this), but if your *why* isn't rooted in your own values and driven by your own pleasure embodiment, it won't be enough to sustain you through the challenges. The key to unlocking the polyamory paradox is your pleasure. Where the four trauma responses have made it difficult to connect with your own desires, pleasure is the antidote. Whether you are feeling lonely and rejected or oversaturated by the emotions of dating multiple people at once, asking pleasure to guide you will help you stay committed to the most important relationship of all, the one with yourself.

PLEASURE OPPRESSION

We live in such hyper-sexualized cultures and subcultures that most of us learned the pleasure-equals-sex primary association pretty early on. Part of this has to do with our avoidance of speaking directly about sex and orgasms; I wish I had a dollar for every time I heard someone refer to pleasure when they actually meant orgasm. And a lot of *that* comes from what pleasure-based business coach Luna Dietrich calls "pleasure oppression."

We live in a world designed by oppressive systems. Pretty much every system of oppression you can think of operates by keeping humans disconnected from their holistic sense of pleasure. Not just that, but their continued existence actually *relies* on those who are oppressed remaining disconnected from their bodies, and our bodies are the vehicles through which we experience pleasure. Global capitalism relies on us being more invested in our jobs than listening to our bodies' needs for rest, relaxation, and healing. Patriarchy centers male pleasure, and goes beyond ignoring women's to tell them it is profoundly confusing and even harmful. For example, we've been fed these cultural narratives that female genital anatomy is a mystery, that the clitoris is "hard to find" and the orgasm gap between men and women somehow makes sense (in hetero relationships, men orgasm 95 percent of the time, whereas women orgasm 65 percent of the time).

Keeping people disconnected specifically from sexual pleasure is an infuriatingly smart tool of oppressive systems, because it teaches us humans to ignore and override our bodies' clearest signals of what we want. When it comes to sex and pleasure, most folx have horrendously poor communication, which has contributed to learning sexual roles that are incredibly limited. These limited roles mean limited intimacy, and intimacy is one of the strongest tools we have in the pursuit of liberation.

When we routinely ignore or learn to quiet the messages we receive from ourselves about what we want, we are more primed to internalize the desires of our context. If we perpetually tell ourselves, "I'm not supposed to want that," or "Keep that desire to yourself – it's shameful," we are inherently more likely to adopt what society tells us to want, like a college education, or a specific salary to support a specific idea of what life is supposed to look like. As a result, we grow up with a very limited view of what romantic and sexual relationships are meant to be.

One of the ways pleasure oppression plays out is through the fawning and people-pleasing tendencies we talked about in the previous chapter. Remember how men are at the top of the pleasure hierarchy in our dominant culture, and everyone else's role in society comes with expectations to be of service to that structure somehow? These embodied stress responses are as common as they are because they are a tool of the patriarchy. These are social survival behaviors that operate by putting our wants, needs, desires and pleasure *after* those of the people around us (or whoever it is we're trying to maintain a safe connection with). Centering their wants and needs not only means that we are routinely sidestepping the pleasure that would support our own optimal functioning, but also that when we notice clearer signals from ourselves about what we do and don't want, we question them. When fawning and people-pleasing have been so central to our social survival, we have conditioned ourselves to believe that our belonging depends upon our service to others. We might unconsciously frame our own wants and needs as at best, not useful to us, and at worst actually dangerous, not to be trusted.

The fear of our own pleasure and insecurity about how to assert it is part of the people-pleasing that shows up in sex. Consider, however, that you must be connected to your pleasure for your partners to trust your "yes." If I say yes to new sexual scenarios without feeling connected to my own desire for them, I am more likely to reflect on them and take issue. Particularly if your non-monogamy involves group sex, you might find yourself questioning whether your hesitation is worth slowing everyone down, or you might be afraid of offending someone in the group who you don't want to engage with. Going along with these scenarios simply not to rock the boat denies the absence of your desire, and can leave you with a feeling like you've actually violated yourself. When you tell your partner about your true experience, it also changes their perception of the experience, and they might question how to know when you really mean "yes."

There are other times in non-monogamy in which your desires and needs may be different from your partners', and choosing your own pleasure may spark feelings in them you'd rather not face. When a last-minute date pops up, it may feel risky or scary to tell your partner, even if all they were planning that night was watching TV. Or if your partner is triggered about someone you're seeing, and asking you to pause those interactions, it may feel like pursuing your own pleasure could cost you your partnership.

RECLAIMING PLEASURE AS MEDICINE

What if you started to replace words like enjoyment and satisfaction with the concept of pleasure? Would that make it easier to understand that it's essential for satisfaction in relationships? Your desire is your power, so long as you believe you are worth fulfilling it.

If you were raised in any industrialized culture of the past several decades (hell, centuries), I can almost guarantee you have a complicated relationship with pleasure. I can also almost guarantee your understanding and experience of pleasure has not been in alignment with our collective wellbeing. Chances are you learned to care more about what people think of you than what you think of them. If you were raised as a cishet woman, chances are you learned you weren't supposed to pursue, but to be chosen. This has variations in the experiences of different genders and sexualities, but the point now is that your sense of choice needs to come back with a vengeance. Reclaiming your pleasure is about reclaiming this agency; you do not need to wait to be chosen and it does not serve you to prioritize being chosen over connecting more deeply with your own felt sense of what *you* like and desire.

When you pursue your true desires, you become the most well-resourced version of yourself. There will be some uncomfortable bumps along the road of this reprogramming, but the most well-resourced version of yourself is the one that can show up in relationships in the most confident, secure, fulfilling way. On a physiological level, reclaiming pleasure is a supportive parallel process to trauma resolution; the health benefits of pleasure help to balance out the physiological stressors of trauma. When our body is responding to a threat, it increases the production of certain hormones like cortisol and adrenaline (let's call them the "pricklies"). When the threat passes, or we get supportive regulation, our body is meant to metabolize that spike of hormones, not keep producing them. Other hormones, like endorphins (let's call these ones the "sparklies") help us to suppress over-producing the pricklies. In short, the more sparklies in your system, the less pricklies, making you a *sparklier* self, partner, and community member. Learning to commit to your pleasure as a resource ripple out to heal your relationships and communities by changing how you interact with others.

Pleasure also drives pro-social behavior and human connection. Sure, if I ask you to think of your primary relationship right now, there might be some big feelings of conflict that come up. But if I ask you to think of the moments you knew you were falling in love, what memories come to mind? I bet those memories feel pretty good. What we call "new relationship energy" floods the body with feel-good neurotransmitters: this is how pleasure bonds us in relationships.

HOLISTIC PLEASURE: THE FOUR REALMS OF BEING HUMAN

You are physiologically designed for pleasure to guide every aspect of your life. We are *designed* for pleasure to be a motivating force not just in our procreation (which is an essentially Darwinist attitude that I'd like us to toss out the window), but in everything we do. Physical pain – i.e., the absence of pleasure, or the unpleasant – is meant to teach us what to avoid, whereas physical pleasure rewards us with neurochemicals that build brain circuits that say, "Do more of that," and support our social engagement system. Pleasure helps our bodies in understanding what to move toward, and also how to do it in connection with other humans. Pleasure, therefore, is a guiding force in building interdependence. But I bet you weren't raised to see it that way. If you were, you probably don't need to be reading this.

When I talk about pleasure, most people immediately

assume I'm talking about sex. And sure, a lot of the time that's a safe assumption. (I do love talking about sex, and thankfully I've built a career that involves quite a bit of that). But to me this assumption highlights just how much our cultural conditioning obfuscates our sensuality, our connection to our bodies. Pleasure is not just about sex, it's about our ability to embody a joyous, connected life. If I ask you to imagine the scent of your favorite flower, the texture of your favorite food on your tongue, the sound of your beloved arriving home after a long trip, the feeling of connection from doing what you love, wouldn't those imaginings also bring up pleasure for you? That's because human pleasure shows up in all realms of our life.

This can be a hard concept to grasp when we've spent decades internalizing that sex is dirty, rest needs to be earned, we are failing if we're not self-sufficient, and worth (including our own) is inherently tied to sacrifice, hard work, and struggle. The framework I teach my clients is something I refer to as a holistic approach to pleasure, meant to help us reclaim its primacy in our lives. A holistic approach to pleasure basically frames it as an integral human experience across four realms of our being: body-based, mental-emotional, spiritual or energetic (depending on whether you identify as spiritual), and relational. When we are more or less balanced across the four realms, we are generally well, happy, and fulfilled. In times of struggle, we will usually find that at least one of the realms of pleasure is lacking.

For you to feel at ease, connected, and confident within your practice of non-monogamy, the most important thing is your own relationship to holistic pleasure. When you are feeling distraught, insecure, or overwhelmed, look to balance your own pleasure just as much as you work on the relationship with another person. You can do that by turning to your four realms:

Body-based pleasure is where we access all the various pleasures of being in a body, experiencing sensory stimulation and sensation information. Each of the five senses is a pleasure avenue. We can experience body-based pleasure through activities like (but not limited to) dancing, sex (whether solo, partnered, or group), non-sexual touch, eating and tasting, smelling, cuddling, taking in colors or visuals we love, body scan meditations…. Body-based pleasure provides important guidance in our connection to pleasure because it is through our body and our sense that we, well, make sense of everything. Our body shows us our preferences, our yeses and noes, our felt sense of want. Body-based pleasure connects us to the truth of what we desire and what we reject. Coming home to body-based pleasure is a process of reclaiming our trust in ourselves, our knowing of our own wisdom and worth. Excavating the shame and guilt that has been placed on body-based pleasure can set us free in so many ways.

Mental-emotional pleasure is where we access intellect, joy, passion, curiosity, play, and perhaps most importantly, purpose. We experience mental-emotional pleasure through activities like (but not limited to) reading, learning, hobbies, meditation, games, conversation, and creative expression. Mental-emotional desire (what we want to learn about or what strikes our curiosity) is important to attune to, as it provides important guidance in supporting our mental-emotional wellbeing. This is also the realm of pleasure where we most often nurture the gifts we have to offer in service of the collective.

Spiritual and energetic pleasure include (but are not limited to) the pleasure available through things like prayer, breathwork, meditation, ritual, plant medicine, sex and BDSM, music and / or sound, and art. We experience spiritual and emotional pleasure through anything that helps us feel the pleasure of connecting to something larger than ourselves. Spiritual and emotional pleasure are important to attune to, as they provide important guidance for our connection to the collective and our place in existence. This kind of pleasure is or can be especially supportive when the world feels overwhelming. It can help us connect to larger hopes and dreams for the well-being of all beings.

Relational pleasure is where we access the pleasure of being in relationship. This can be relationship with others, with nature, with pets or animal beings, and importantly, with self. We can experience relational pleasure through activities like (but not limited to) journaling, sex (whether solo, partnered, or group), conversation, dancing, cooking meals, cuddles, creative collaboration, reading, playing games, time in nature, activism and community organizing, eye gazing, and other forms of co-regulating. Relational pleasure provides important guidance in supporting our individual selves, but also our communities and networks. Relational pleasure is perhaps the most important component of this pleasure framework, because it is the realm through which we move beyond pleasure as an individualistic practice. Relational pleasure is how we root into self-love free from internalized oppression, and also helps us practice pleasure in ways that embody values like interdependence, collaboration, and justice despite oppressive contexts.

YOUR FOUR REALMS OF PLEASURE

Let's brain dump your four realms of pleasure. Looking at how you've related to them generally in your life can (1) help you see that you have an existing relationship with each, even if this feels like a foreign concept, and (2) give you a resource list to draw from when you find yourself lacking in one. So grab some paper and a pen, and under each category, write down as many things as you can think of that have given you the experience of that kind of pleasure.

It's OK if the same thing shows up in multiple realms. For example, for me, sometimes dancing is about the pleasure of connecting to my body, sometimes it is a pleasurable spiritual experience, sometimes it is the perfect mental-emotional pleasure to act as an anxiety antidote, and it is also a vehicle for relational pleasure, sometimes with myself and sometimes with others. Which category it falls under depends on the more specific context. Right now, we're just doing a general brain dump to help the brain orient to the pleasure that already exists, and to give ourselves a guide for noticing our glimmers.

After this brain dump, look over your lists: Which realms of pleasure feel easier for you to access? Which feel less present? If you see a glaring imbalance, that immediately tells us where we want to nurture your pleasure first. That could mean simply expanding your awareness of this realm of pleasure, or the definitions of what count in that realm. It could mean you commit to a daily or weekly or monthly practice of something that connects you to that realm.

In more acute moments of challenge, taking stock of your four realms can be illuminating of where you need to take action or strike balance. For example, my client Sara and I had been working on sexual pleasure and her open relationship with Angel for a few months when she got on a call and said, "I'm feeling great about where we've gotten with the sex and sexuality stuff, but I'm still getting upset with Angel for reasons I'm not fully clear about. I feel this intense anger toward them and dissatisfaction. I get triggered whenever they go on a date, even though we've made agreements that feel good to me and they're meeting all of them." She elaborated on some intense feelings of anger, being underappreciated, and feeling like her work context was a "fucked-up trap." We did a four-realms check in, noting how she'd experienced each over the past couple of weeks. I wanted to know where her *pleasure* was undernourished. Small irritations or frustrations can turn into big triggers if we can't access well-rounded pleasure.

We quickly found that her pathways of mental-emotional pleasure were basically offline; she told me she didn't really have any examples of truly *feeling* mental-emotional pleasure in the past few weeks. When this is the case, we first ask ourselves: what can I do to nurture this pleasure? And we refer back to the brain dump you just made. Go straight to whatever you wrote down for that realm of pleasure, and do whatever sounds most appealing in the current moment. Repeat every day, maybe multiple times a day.

For Sara, the lack of mental-emotional pleasure felt weird to acknowledge because she had been going through the actions of things that usually brought her that (reading, meditating, drawing). So then the questions we ask the body are:

- What different activities or practices in that realm feel easier or more pleasurable right now?
- Is there something standing in the way of receiving this kind of pleasure? Do I have any power to address that blockage?

It may take some time to truly move back toward balance, and it may require help from others, but this is one of the best ways we can take ownership of our own pleasure and fulfilment. And though we are pursuing interdependence in non-monogamy, an important part of interdependence operating smoothly is each person taking appropriate responsibility for their own wellbeing.

Sara came back two weeks later saying she'd addressed the blockage, which was unreasonable stress from work. The next time Angel was on a date with someone else, Sara filled the time with different things that brought her mental-emotional pleasure. And when Angel came home, she was happy to see them.

GLIMMERS

Triggers are the things that take us outside the window of tolerance. Glimmers are the exact opposite; they are whatever experiences support us staying within our window of tolerance. They are delicious hugs from your besties. They are laughing with your partner over something only the two of you find funny. They are noticing that your body is relaxed again after a post-work yoga session. Glimmers are all the things that help us access both our social nervous system and our "rest and digest" functions in the body. In what I teach, pleasure equals glimmer.

As long as you are alive, you have a body in some form. Pleasure is something we experience through the body, simply because everything we experience as humans is something we interpret through these bony meat sacks full of electrical signals. I'm not poo-poohing energetics and spirituality, by any means. But so long as you are existing in this lifetime in your human body, that's your vehicle for making sense of information. What this means is that regardless of which realm of pleasure we're talking about, the experience of that pleasure has an impact on your body. And where in earlier chapters we talked about the impacts of trauma on the body, pleasure basically has the opposite effect. Pleasure in any of the four realms supports the nervous system's optimal functioning in the social engagement system, and also supports our capacity for resilience.

We have a lot of neural circuitry that is predisposed for seeing the bad and putting us on alert. In order to expand our window of tolerance and our capacity for loving social connection, it helps to strengthen the neural pathways that attune us to what is good, what is working, what feels supportive. When we are in intense, scary places, like watching our partner catch feelings for someone we don't know, that concept can feel pretty far out of reach, but even simply setting the intention to notice glimmers more regularly can have a profound impact.

In my work, I call this "pleasure orienting;" we don't need to make a huge effort to pursue feelings of goodness that are actually outside our current capacity (which will likely lead to disappointment, frustration, and in extreme cases, toxic shame), but simply to orient ourselves to whatever pleasure is *already* accessible. Over time, the practices of pleasure orienting will strengthen our baseline attunement to pleasure. Ultimately, pleasure orienting helps us expand the window of tolerance, thereby enhancing our capacity for connection, problem solving, restoration of physical body, empathy, and even more pleasure.

These are the two fundamental practices I introduce to most clients:

FIVE SENSES ORIENTING

This is a brief sensory check-in, usually in a seated position, but can be done in any position that is comfortable (including walking). It's not important if you're still or moving, the goal is to be in a condition in which you can bring awareness to each of the five senses. Eyes can be open or closed, whichever feels more inviting to you. I also acknowledge that for some of us, each of the five senses may be accessible in different capacities – this is wonderful. If it is particularly unenjoyable or upsetting for you to bring awareness to one of your senses, remember you have permission to skip anything that doesn't work for you. That may be something to explore in the presence of a coach, therapist, or a friend who can help you regulate.

Begin by noticing where you are in space, acknowledging where you are in relation to the walls, ceiling, floor, furniture, etc. (or if outside, the sky, plants, buildings, road, etc.)

Next, notice where the different parts of your body are in relation to each other, noting where you sense your legs, your arms, your torso, your head.

If it feels OK for you, you might begin to invite some awareness to the breath; noticing its pace, its depth, its movement in the torso. (If it is feeling fast / constricted, try humming with your exhale to help it slow down.)

Then slowly move awareness through each of the five senses. Spend as long as you like with each, but I usually start with three to five breath cycles. I like to go in the order of hearing, seeing, smelling, tasting, touching, but you can do whatever feels right for you.

Notice the *experience* of the sense, rather than labeling the source of the sound or smell or the object you see.

Rather, what does it *feel* like in your body for you to be engaging this sense?

Then notice if you can access any pleasure from this sense, in this present moment. Notice what it feels like (in the language of the body) for you to intentionally receive that pleasure.

Finally, take a moment to try to engage the pleasure of all five together. If it feels OK to focus on breath, take one to three cycles of breath; inhale filling all five senses with pleasure; exhale *audibly* sighing out anything that isn't feeling pleasurable to the body.

PLEASURE REFLECTIONS

This is a bedtime list, ideally written daily, of the pleasures you experienced in your day.

- Before going to bed (toward the very end of your day – can be the last thing you do), take a moment to tune into your body. Ask it to remind you about all the pleasure you experienced over the course of the day.
- Write down everything that comes to mind.
- See if you can note at least one thing for each realm of pleasure. Remember, it's OK if one thing counts for more than one realm! (We're just asking you to build the mental muscle of remembering that these realms exist and that yes, you have access to them)

Bonus points for beginners: the smaller the better! In both exercises, paradoxically, pleasure orienting is more effective the smaller the pleasures you train yourself to see. The more the body trains itself to receive the small stuff, the easier it becomes to access our glimmers even when we are struggling or approaching the limit of our window of tolerance. Over time, tuning in for the teeniest, tiniest signals of pleasure becomes second nature, and your baseline returns to / becomes far more regulated than before.

Pleasure Values

Defining our values is a great way to gain clarity in our pursuit of holistic pleasure. When we know what our values are, our energy flows with more ease to the places and relationships where we experience a sense of living in alignment with our values. These spaces and relationships are more deeply satisfying to us, and as a result, we experience them as more pleasurable. As you open up, it will be helpful to understand where to turn and which relationships to nurture in order to stay in integrity with your own values. Part of the transition we're making is away from the monogamous default that our one-partner relationship fills all those expressions of our truth. You need to know what will make you feel good, fulfilled, and satisfied outside of that single relationship, and defining your values can be a massively helpful tool in that orienting.

Defining Your Values

First, make a list of all the values you feel you embody (see below for some examples to get the ball rolling). Make sure to include ones related to your pleasure (like self-care, rest, sexual expression, etc.).

Examples of values: accountability, adaptability, adventure, affection, anti-capitalism, authenticity, balance, beauty, bravery, calmness, community, compassion, collaboration, creativity, curiosity, determination, dignity, diversity, empathy, enthusiasm, environmentalism, ethics, expression, exploration, faith, friendship, fun, generosity, gratitude, growth, happiness, health, humor, honesty, imagination, innovation, integrity, intelligence, interdependence, justice, kindness, knowledge, learning, liberation, love, loyalty, newness, openness, optimism, organization, originality, passion, patience, peace, playfulness, power, purpose, respect, self-actualization, sensitivity, service, sex-positivity, sincerity, solidarity, spirituality, strength, success, sustainability, teamwork, transparency, trust, understanding, uniqueness, wealth, wisdom.

Review the list and cross out any that were driven by the internal thought "this *should* be one of my values" or that doesn't actually feel aligned to you right now. (This can always change down the road.)

Star the top three to five that you feel you've been embodying or guided by in the past year. Write a sentence or two (or more) about what that looks like for you: How have you been putting these values into action? How does that feel?

Circle the top three to five you want to nurture in this transition to non-monogamy (yes, it's OK if the values overlap with the ones from the past year). Write a sentence or two (or more) about how you would *love* for these values to be expressed in your life. How does non-monogamy give you an opportunity to put these values into practice? How can these values be embodied and guide your actions? How can you receive pleasure from practicing these values?

When we think of what happens on a physiological level when we experience pleasure, we get to understand it as a resource that supports us. Understanding what brings you pleasure across your four realms first acts as your toolkit for calming yourself amidst major triggers. With time and practice, building your relationship with your own pleasure helps you build your secure attachment to yourself, so external triggers become less ... well, triggering. Pleasure practice roots you into your own self-worth, your embodied knowing that not only do you deserve to have your desires fulfilled, but that it is possible to have your desires fulfilled. With time, it also expands your creativity and intuition in how to get your needs met in multiple other ways outside of this central partnership, thereby creating more freedom for the both of you.

Your pleasure will teach you that what you want *is* there for you. When we balance our pleasure well across the four realms, and understand the embodiment of our values as something that grants us pleasure, we expand into our full capacity for right relationship with ourselves and with others. As we'll see in the chapters ahead, centering pleasure supports how we are able to address challenges.

If you want some help leveraging your pleasure as a resource in your regulation tools and practices, check out the link provided at the back of the book. I made you a class that comes with a worksheet.

7

THE POLYAMORY PARADOX

"I want this but I feel like I'm going to die."

— CLEMENTINE MORRIGAN

"Love rests on two pillars: surrender and autonomy. Our need for togetherness exists alongside our need for separateness. One does not exist without the other."

— ESTHER PEREL

The paradox most of us face in the process of opening up is that while we are maintaining or developing a deep, intimate bond with someone, we are also consensually participating in dynamics that can cause us to feel rejected or abandoned by that same person. And not just once or twice as a circumstance of life, but as an inherent component of what we have consciously structured with them. For anybody, there is obviously a conundrum here. For those with developmental trauma, complex-PTSD, or who identify with disorganized attachment, this can mimic the feelings of childhood, in which caregivers were unreliable and we became conditioned to tolerate mistreatment and / or emotional neglect. The paradox for folx who identify as non-monogamous and have trauma in their backgrounds is often that they really desire this relationship format, *and* the triggers in it can be unbearable. So, in this chapter, we will explore the very nature of relationships so that we can better nurture our sense of connection, even as we change the circumstances of the relationship. Understanding how we make meaning with our loved ones gives us more power to practice pleasure with them rather than succumbing to forces of disconnection.

MEANING-MAKING

Intimacy is a web spun of shared meaning. As we reveal more and more of ourselves to the people in our lives, and as we go through various experiences with them, we build a lexicon of activities, behaviors, jokes, reference points, understandings of each other's pasts and current contexts that all contribute to our sense of knowing each other. Where we have intimacy is where we feel someone knows what is specifically meaningful to us, or where we have constructed meaning together. We create shared meaning through rituals, roles, goals, and symbols. To feel secure in any relationship, shared meaning is instrumental. If we are struggling to feel secure in a non-monogamous relationship, becoming more conscious and intentional about how we connect to meaning can be transformative. This chapter will go over some key areas of meaning-making in relationship so you can better understand how to leverage them for stronger connection.

The paradox of being in partnership (again, this can

include with ourselves) is that we desire *known* intimacy in order to feel secure, but also yearn for *novelty* to infuse us with vitality and to continue expanding our sense of intimacy. Novel experiences show us new things about ourselves and our partners, and in doing so, give us more material for our sense of knowing and being known. How we process novel experiences with each other then constructs our shared meaning. Like that trip that was supposed to be a romantic getaway where absolutely everything went wrong – now you look back on it and laugh about how you could have possibly ended up eating cotton candy at a local fair at two in the morning. Sure, you had to move hotels twice, and never found the quiet part of the beach everyone told you to visit, but it taught you a lot about how each of you problem-solves when you don't speak the language. In the moment, it forced you to work together in new ways. And as you were strolling down the streets looking for dinner, you shared observations about what made that place so different from home. Now, in addition to the trust you built, neither of you looks at cotton candy the same way anymore.

Part of the destabilization of opening up is that it inevitably challenges our sense of established shared meaning in a relationship, even a relationship with ourselves. Or, if you're making this transition into a new relationship, any meaning you *assumed* was shared when looking for monogamous relationships is thrown out. It's easy for the rituals, roles, goals, and symbols that we translate as "security" to feel like they've been sacrificed entirely for novelty (even if that is technically not the case). But we need both. So what is meaningful to us, what matters in the relationship, must be clearly defined anew.

Again, this is a big concept, but I invite you to start small: What shared meaning have you recently accessed with your partner that you didn't even think about at the time? Did you put on your favorite show after dinner without discussion? One of you called the other by a nickname only you know the origin of? What are the things that happen on autopilot? More specifically, what are the things that happen on autopilot that bring a sense of tenderness, warmth, and affection when you summon them now?

My invitation is to think about this chapter through the lens of what polyamorous therapist Jessica Fern calls "expressed delight." In her HEARTS model for building securely attached polyamorous relationships, she explains that expressing delight toward your partners is imperative in supporting the paradigm shift from monogamy (i.e., "I am with you because you're the only one for me") to non-monogamy (i.e., "I'm with you because you are special and unique, but not the only one"). Expressed delight helps us with creating shared meaning because it gives us information about our role(s) in someone's life and can inform our rituals, goals, and symbols. Needing to know the ways in which we are important or spark joy for our partner is not needy or insecure, but an important way of building intimacy and focusing on pleasure to connect us, as opposed to fear, conflict, and fawning.

SMALL-BUT-MIGHTY MOMENTS

Small-but-mighty moments are the glimmers in a relationship between two or more people. All the teeniest, tiniest behaviors, gestures, rituals, and symbols that speak to what is unique in your connection. As Deb Dana says, "A glimmer can be a micro-moment that's predictably present in your world." I call them small-but-mighty, because they often sound somewhat insignificant on their own, without the context of the relationship, but in the context of the relationship, they have the power to drastically shift things for the worse or the better. It's in the small things that the majority of intimacy is established and maintained. Yes, we create shared meaning through big, transformational things, but the maintenance of ongoing connection happens in the mundane.

Some examples of small-but-mighty moments:

- Texting goodnight or good morning
- Sharing a meal
- A six-second kiss or six-minute cuddle
- Squeezing a partner's leg / hand / shoulder when you notice a conversation at a dinner party making them uncomfortable
- Bringing partner their favorite coffee to get them out of bed
- That specific way they like to be touched or teased during sex
- An unexpected gift
- Leaving a Post-It note with a heart on it for your partner when you leave for work
- Watching a show or listening to a podcast together
- Going for walks
- Unsolicited acts of service
- Pet names
- Inside jokes
- Silly sounds or made-up songs / phrases you came up with together
- The "attachment gaze" as Diane Poole Heller calls the warm, happy, way we stare at someone when we're in love

- Communicating something you've observed that makes your partner feel seen

The small-but-mighty moments are the foundation upon which we build roles and goals, and can easily fall to the wayside in early non-monogamy, especially if one partner is becoming consumed with a new relationship and overcome by what we call "new relationship energy" (NRE). When we are getting the small-but-mighty moments we're used to, it's easier to feel secure in our place in our partners' life because we are receiving feedback that has a shared meaning of our importance. When a partner is more distracted, less attentive, perhaps away more often and getting easily sucked into their phone even when they are with us, we start to feel a decline in the small-but-mighty moments. This can make it hard to feel secure in our own role in the partnership, but can also cause us to call our partner's role in our life into question – "What is their role if I can't rely on them for the emotional security I once did?"

Think about it this way: you're in the midst of a family crisis and could really use your partner's support in going to visit family during a stressful time, as has been one of their roles in your life for the past few years. If, in the days leading up to this visit, you are missing the normal small-but-mighty moments, having your partner with you in this role may not feel as helpful as you'd hoped. If they have been in NRE and going on dates while you fret about your family, it may feel like the role of supporting you has all but disappeared, right? And this can feel *really* confusing because so much of what we've read about non-monogamy is to not be co-dependent, right? We're supposed to let people have other experiences and not try to attach them to our own emotional states, right? But then what do we do about needing emotional support?

Now, the magic power of small-but-mighty moments comes from our attunement to the unique individual in front of us. We can bring our partner a coffee in the morning, but if we brought the drink our *other* girlfriend likes, we have mis-attuned. Rather than this being received as a nice gesture, it could easily backfire if the interpreted meaning is that the coffee-carrying partner was thinking more about someone else, and not about the partner in front of them.

So back to the question of needing emotional support: recognizing even a few of the small-but-mighty moments that help you feel seen and supported gives you the power to ask for those gestures. And these requests of your partner do not have to change the fact that they are in NRE or have the impact of dragging them into something more painful. It's actually a wonderful way to request what you need and give your partner an opportunity to recognize where they can express their care for you in the most effective ways.

This can also translate into creating rituals for coming back together after dates with other people. For example, if you feel particularly connected to your partner through sharing food and physical touch, it might be a good fit for your relationship to request that when they are coming home from a night with someone else, they bring you breakfast and spend ten minutes cuddling before you discuss the date or go about your day. Clients sometimes resist this, protesting that if they have to ask for it, the gesture doesn't feel genuine. But I say what have you actually got to lose? If you feel making specific requests cheapens your partner's care, you can also give them a few options and ask them to choose on their own. Regardless of what the content is, following through on the commitment to re-connect through small-but-mighty moments can work wonders.

The same is true when it comes to conflict or deep emotional processing. If you are feeling really disconnected from each other, or watching your body move into stress, going for a walk to "your spot" or dancing to your favorite album together can be great stress interrupters that also remind you of your positive feelings for each other.

SHARED MISSION

The shared mission of the relationship is where your pleasure and your partner's pleasure overlap and support your mutual pleasure. It is what you agree to prioritize together. Now, that doesn't mean you have to want exactly the same things or make the same meaning from shared experiences. But shared mission is where your agreements and commitments to each other can be fulfilled with a sense of ease because they are rooted in pleasure. This is a particularly important concept to touch on in opening up, because we are all handed a default shared mission in the dominant monogamy culture: build a monogamous life that involves children. To be clear, that's not a bad mission. It's just that when you move away from it, feeling secure might depend on knowing what you're moving toward.

One way to identify shared mission is by comparing notes on your values. If you or your partner(s) didn't do the values exercise already, go back and fill it out individually. Then put your lists together and see if you have any of the same things listed. If yes, discuss how those values are expressed and embodied in your relationship.

Or, if you both have an understanding of your individual mission in the world, it might be worth a conversation about if and how they overlap. Where they overlap, how might you come together to collaborate?

Another way to identify your shared mission is to revisit the exercise from Chapter 6 on your four realms of pleasure, not as individuals, but as a couple, triad, or moresome. How does this relationship access each of the four realms of pleasure in a way that is different than how you access that pleasure as individuals? What's the relationship's list of the four realms of pleasure if we think about it as its own entity? In this version of the exercise, you may find you're listing fewer things than when you did your individual brain dump – that's OK. It may actually be helpful in honing in on the shared mission.

You might find the four realms are way more skewed doing this for a relationship than for an individual. That is also OK. That may simply mean that the shared mission relates to that realm. This can be a sticky spot de-conditioning from non-monogamy because it asks us to confront however we've internalized, "Your partner is your everything." Your shared mission with this person may be much more limited than you thought, *and that's OK!!* It means we are one step closer to helping you build a well-balanced, pleasurable existence. That awareness can help you orient to the other partners you want to call in. For example, when I started getting serious with my partner, a lot of the shared mission was spiritual-energetic, and secondarily physical. This guided me to intentionally seek out other partners who filled a more mental-emotional role for me.

Shared mission helps us understand what objectives are aligned for the relationship, as well as comprehending our roles in each other's lives. Just like a mission statement for an organization, a shared mission can act as our north star when we sense we've gone adrift. A common shared mission in opening up is to support each other's sexual discovery, or to be working toward a certain structure of non-monogamy together. If, for example, the shared mission is to move toward kitchen table polyamory, the goals of the couple will probably relate to developing emotional literacy, learning about what's involved in that kind of structure, and focusing on dating people who are also aligned in that way.

If, however, the mutual holistic pleasure of the partnership is mostly in the life they've established as successful professionals co-habiting and raising children (while exploring group sex together), the shared mission might be more along the lines of "raise our children to be happy adults and live a fulfilling, sexually adventurous life while we do so." The goals for opening up here will be different, of course, because this partnership's mission is not related to changing its structure the same way as the couple pursuing kitchen table polyamory.

The anchor of a shared mission can also help us with distress tolerance and / or integrating dysregulation when we are triggered or jealous by moving our awareness to something larger than ourselves.

THE UNSOLVABLE PROBLEMS WE CHOOSE: INTIMATE PARTNERSHIP AS PARADOX

In her book *Mating in Captivity*, renowned psychotherapist and relationship expert Esther Perel asks us to look at the paradoxes of our relationships as opportunities to practice surrender, as opposed to viewing them as endless problems to be solved. For example, we live amidst the paradox that long-term love requires closeness, while desire needs some distance. Or how about the fact that romantic satisfaction seems to require a certain level of frustration in the relationship? In fact, there are not endless problems to solve to be in the partnerships we want, just the problem of surrendering to living in paradox.

The Gottman Institute further highlights this idea with the data that 69 percent of relationship problems do not have a solution. Instead, we might think of them as a window into whatever that couples' paradox is. (The language Gottman uses is "perpetual problems" versus "solvable problems.") Solvable problems are purely situational, whereas perpetual problems stem from our deep differences, either in personality or lifestyle. Perpetual problems are how we learn to care for each other, because they demand what is necessary to stay in connection despite challenge; we must learn to dance together in and around conflict with grace, humor, acknowledgment, and respect.

Solvable problems are contextual, usually things that simply require changing a circumstance or gaining a new skill set, like communicating differently. Unsolvable problems are more like Itai needs to tour for the sake of his career, mental health, and soul, but this is triggering for Irene, and that trigger impacts her mental health and career negatively. As you can see from this example, unsolvable problems could also be seen as mismatched needs.

Another aspect of opening up that contributes to our total melting down is the paradigm shift in which we haven't yet learned what is solvable versus what is perpetual in this new relational structure. Is it a solvable or unsolvable problem if my partner falls in love with someone I don't like? Is it a solvable or unsolvable problem that one of us wants casual sex and the other wants kitchen table poly? Figuring out what is solvable and what is not is one of the keys to our freedom in any relationship, in part because it helps us tap back into our agency in a nuanced and healthy way (as opposed to being avoidant or controlling).

Opening up will show the cracks where assumptions and poor communication have built themselves a comfy home in your relationship (and yourself). If you have taken the avoidance approach to your particular unsolvable conflict as opposed to developing supportive coping mechanisms and working on your empathy and communication around it, whatever that pain point is may surface with a vengeance.

When we take away the security we felt from the structure of monogamy, what insecurities are staring back at us? For me, there was an unexpected answer here; I'd been operating with the unconscious assumption that I could be in long-term relationships without getting my own needs met, forever prioritizing my partners' comfort and desires, securing my belonging by being "of service" to them. For many of my clients, this also rings true. But is this a solvable problem or an unsolvable problem?

In *The Subtle Art of Not Giving a Fuck*, Mark Manson introduces us to the idea that we never reach the end of problem-solving, but that a solution to one problem simply provides us with new problems. Our satisfaction in life, he claims, comes from solving the problems we have chosen to solve. Part of how we can set ourselves up for success is by choosing the problems wisely. If we can choose to view the problem of unsolvable problems as a problem of our own surrender, then we can find the satisfaction we thought we wanted by solving the unsolvable. If we can learn about our central conflicts and unsolvable problems, we give ourselves the opportunity to choose a better problem. And by "better" I mean one we can solve:

how to communicate and collaborate better (which we'll explore in the coming chapters).

For starters, we can try approaching them through the lens of pleasure....

PLEASURE-BASED RITUALS FOR APPROACHING THE UNSOLVABLE

In lieu of being able to resolve a paradox, we want to be able to find connection within it. This means consciously countering the tendencies to become defensive or accusatory. When you find yourself in the space of "I can't believe it's this same thing again," or "They *always* do this," or "They *never* do that," get out of your head and into your "animal body." When my partner and I have been apart and / or with someone else, the first thing we do is get back in our bodies together. Ideally, this happens through either a sense of play or rest or exploration. This can be play wrestling (actually pretending to be animals), physical contact like cuddling for six minutes, or going for a sensory walk.

If you're feeling angry, confused, or conflicted about being vulnerable, try something that feels good but doesn't involve eye contact. This could be sitting back-to-back and breathing in sync, focusing awareness on each other's breath. Or this could be closing your eyes and taking turns giving each other massage on a specific part of the body. Refer back to your relationship's pleasure inventory for ideas.

If you're triggered, try to choose a pleasure ritual that meets that realm of nervous system activation. For example, if you can recognize fight or flight, have a dance party together. How does the anger or self-protection want to be communicated with your body?

If you're going more toward freeze or shutdown, how about some cuddling on the couch to re-establish safety with each other? Is there a part of your body that always likes to be massaged? Can you and your partner exchange six-minute gentle massages? Or quietly drink a cup of tea while back-to-back and breathing into each other's bodies?

Pleasure orienting is another tool we can apply to solving our relationship with the unsolvable. When we practice pleasure orienting, there are two questions to ask:

1. What pleasure am I currently already able to access?
2. What pleasure *might* I receive from this experience?

The first can be a simple five senses scan, as detailed in Chapter 6. This serves to regulate the body and subconsciously remind you that you are OK in the here and now. The second can help us hold space for both / and while we move through challenging feelings. I went through this a lot with compersion. I *might* glean relational pleasure from knowing my partner is getting their needs met; I *might* glean emotional pleasure from the growth of learning more specifically what I want and what I need to ask for; I *might* even glean body-based pleasure from recognizing the very thing triggering me is also turning me on. (Caveat: this orienting is not to be used for gaslighting yourself or trying to make sexual pleasure out of something that causes you pain.)

8

WHAT THEY SAID VERSUS WHAT YOU HEARD

"Without knowing one another, we can never experience intimacy."

— BELL HOOKS

F irst of all, give yourself tons and tons and tons of time. The transition from monogamy to non-monogamy will reveal *all* the places where you might need to work on communication, and for 99 percent of us, that is a lot.

Get cozy with the expectation that you *will* have miscommunications – that is a part of this process. You will discover your partner doesn't know certain things about you, where maybe you assumed they did. You will discover things about your partner you weren't expecting. They will discover things about themselves they weren't expecting, and so will you. What do you need in order to more easily accept miscommunication as part of the process? It's good to ponder this a little bit ahead of time, so you can remind yourself when it arises.

Add on top of that all the things about non-monogamy that create extra hurdles to your old ways of communicating, and you might be in for a doozy of a communication up-level. Some of the deconditioning from toxic monogamy culture is facing the fact that communicating a feeling is not the same as making a request or an agreement. In compulsory monogamy culture, because our partner is positioned to be our entire relational universe in a hyper-romanticized way, it comes with the expectation that they will get to know us without us having to articulate every little thing about ourselves. We expect them to see us and "get us" in our entirety. Of course, this doesn't work no matter what kind of relationship you're in, but the miscommunication that comes with it in non-monogamy can result in the very specific pain of watching your partner do things with other people that you thought you didn't consent to. The number one thing I hear from clients struggling in non-monogamy is: "I can't believe my partner doesn't see / understand this part of me. I can't believe they thought I would be OK with that." Whenever I hear this, I know we need to talk about communication.

We each come to relationships making different assumptions about what it means to love well. When we experience rupture, it often points us to a place where those assumptions are different than our partners'. What if we can re-frame that feeling of not being seen as an opportunity to show them? Communication is the key to teaching each other how we want to be loved.

MISCOMMUNICATION

Early on in my non-monogamy I somewhat accidentally found myself in a kinky threesome with someone my partner had introduced me to. We'll call him Dan. While my partner was in a different country, in a time zone with an eight-hour difference from me, this acquaintance invited me to join him and his mistress, Ashley, for dinner. Dinner came with an invitation to stay the night in the same hotel as them, and eventually was also paired with an offer for a massage therapist to come to the room after our meal. An Uber black was sent to collect me from my apartment, nearly an hour away from the restaurant. I was intoxicated by the swank, the thrill of so clearly being desired, but also the exhilaration of the open nature of the whole thing.

In all of my conversations with my partner leading up to the dinner, I heard some trepidation from him, and I assured him that I wasn't interested in sex with this acquaintance (which was true in my more traditional, vanilla, monogamous sensibilities). He told me that me getting into any kind of sexual situation with the two of them was not his preference, but that if that was the outcome of the night, "Of course, we will figure it out." I told him that while I wasn't sexually drawn to Dan, I was curious to learn more about BDSM, so I could see a scenario in which they opened the door to let me play and I declined but wound up watching instead.

Fast forward to the hotel room later, in which my arms are tied behind my back, I'm furiously licking Ashley's pussy, and they're taking turns putting the Hitachi to my clit. How did I get here, you might ask, after so adamantly assuring my partner, I wasn't attracted to Dan? Well, there are a few things at play, but the one that's relevant to the chapter on communication is that my own people-pleasing kept me from communicating my truth ahead of time. I didn't yet trust that I could be affirmed in my relationship stating a desire different from my partner's, so I minimized what I might have wanted to lean into.

Also, important to note that I didn't yet have the experience to know that I can be kink-attracted to someone without being sexually attracted to them. It is actually somewhat rare for me to be both sexually and kink-attracted. I didn't have any frame of reference for the fact that I might want more in the kink dynamic with Dan than I would imagine wanting in a sexual dynamic with him. So my assurance to my partner wasn't unfounded, it was just misguided.

The experience blew my mind, opened a completely new sexual channel in me. But it also triggered Ashley, and we wound down the scene in a rather abrupt way that left me without significant aftercare. I went to my own room, somewhat delirious, and looking for connection. I calculated the time difference between me and my partner, realized he would be up, and opened my video chat. When I began to dive into all the unexpected antics right off the bat, he interrupted me with: "Whoa, Irene, what?! I thought we agreed you weren't going to get involved. You directly went against what I asked for. I can't believe you did this."

"Whoa, what?! I thought you said, 'Whatever happens, we'll figure it out.' I don't remember you saying this was off limits for you."

What proceeded was a long, messy, somewhat devastating process of repair that took him cutting his trip short, flying back around the world to squeeze in an in-person visit before his next gig, and us taking a long hard look at how our relationship had been operating. *He was shocked to discover that I wasn't happy or fulfilled, and I was shocked to find out that he didn't know that I was struggling as much as I was.*

Some key takeaways from this story:

Most of us struggle to communicate that we're struggling. Regardless of non-monogamy or not, communicating that we're unhappy can come with a lot of shame, especially if the people around us don't have the same struggle. This is extra, extra true of people-pleasers. We will often use what's going on in a partner's life as a reason to "not bother them" with our own stuff. My partner traveling and being excited about the things happening in his life became a crutch for me not wanting to interrupt to say, "I'm having a shit time," and potentially make him feel bad. I also see this in clients when their partner is stressed out and they don't want to add to the strife.

I also wasn't communicating where I was at along the way, in part because I thought committing to an open relationship meant taking sole responsibility for *all* my feelings. And I thought *that* meant the ones that were envious or upset about "stupid" things or feeling unwanted were just mine to deal with on my own, not to share with my partner. But there's a big difference between my feelings being my responsibility and keeping them to myself. Supportive partnership actually depends on keeping your partner in the loop about how you're feeling. (It doesn't mean they have to feel the same way, but will help make sure that the space between you is honest and rooted in reality.)

Making requests of our partners is fucking hard, but very necessary. "I'd rather you didn't" is not an agreement. It's not a request. It's simply a preference, a feeling. Communicating our feelings is 1000% necessary, but it is a different step than making agreements. In a culture that tells men to suppress all their feelings, tells women they are too needy, and doesn't acknowledge that other genders even exist, we all have our deep-rooted reasons why making specific requests can be hard. Most of us have internalized either that we're not supposed to in the first place, or that if we do, we will be harshly rejected. Making requests communicates that we have needs, and also exposes us to the possibility of being rejected.

Having clear agreements is a vital part of non-monogamous intimacy. Without clear agreements, each partner will default to their unique assumptions and ways of operating. If we want to take good care of each other, and be cared for in return, we need clarity about what that means to each person.

KEYS TO COMMUNICATING

You know the saying, "It's not what you say, but how you say it?" According to research from the Gottman Institute, "Ninety-six percent of the time, you can predict the outcome of a conversation based on the first three minutes of the interaction." (Gottman Institute: https://www. gottman.com/blog/the-6-things-that-predict-divorce/). And this is one of the reliable predictors of divorce, or the dissolving of a long-term intimate partnership. So let's discuss how to communicate what you really mean, and also how to listen so you're hearing what your partners mean.

Now, effective communication in intimate relationships requires a few key components:

- *The capacity to listen and be impacted by what you are hearing (i.e., attunement and receptivity):* This means not only listening to the specific words, but for your partner's state of being and cues of the context (*cough*cough* attunement!).

Remember the somatic listening exercise in Chapter 5? It was prepping you for this, because if you aren't tuning in to how you are responding to the discussion, you're probably not fully connected to the content of it.

- *Presence:* Minimizing distractions and offering your focus and attention not only helps you put your thoughts together coherently. It also helps your partner *feel* they are being heard, which supports the next point.

- *Vulnerability:* For us to do hard things together, we have to be able to share hard feelings. When self-protection enters the scene, effective communication runs and hides. This requires enough emotional safety in the relationship for each person to share parts of themselves that might be sensitive, fearful, or hurt. Without doing so, our partner may be operating from a place of assuming our inner experience, not realizing essential truths about your needs. What are you assuming your partner understands? You may be interpreting rejection and hurt where they may be able to interact differently if given the chance to know the truth. You need to be able to be truly vulnerable, and you also need to be able to create safety for their vulnerability.

- *Time:* That means both *enough* time to address sensitive matters, and structured time so you're not drowning in emotional loops that don't go anywhere.

- *Emotional literacy:* This is the ability to identify, understand, communicate, and respond to emotions, both in ourselves and in others. Recall that emotions are signals at the body level. Our ability to sense these signals is called "interoception." Unsurprisingly, interoception is linked to emotional well-being. Increased interoceptive sensitivity (as is common in certain kinds of neurodivergence) is thought to contribute to emotional dysregulation.

HURDLES TO COMMUNICATION

Many of the psychological hurdles to communication are actually our attempts to control unpleasant emotional experiences. We might refrain from telling a partner something we think will upset them because we don't want to feel responsible for that pain. Or worse, we fear if we confront a partner about a way they hurt us, it will require hours of emotional labor trying to get validation and in the end, they'll disregard us anyway, leaving us feeling even worse. Sometimes the known pain feels safer than risking vulnerability. But if we want relationships that support us and are driven by holistic pleasure, we need to learn to identify and address the following in ourselves:

- Fear of confrontation
- Anticipating partner's response: One of the insidious impacts of fawning is that once it's engrained, we are often anticipating the response to our expression as an integral part of assessing how we feel. This interferes with our clarity on what the feeling is in the first place.
- Mis-labeling emotions
- Fear of rejection
- Fear of failure or disappointing a loved one
- Feelings of over-responsibility; poor boundaries around what's mine and what's yours

- Shame about what we're feeling or wanting to request
- Lack of resources

NOT EVERYTHING IS JEALOUSY

Early in non-monogamy, it makes sense that any big, new (or at least increasing in frequency) feelings would be perceived as jealousy. In monogamy culture, we are more likely to deal with jealousy by controlling the trigger for it; if husband is jealous of wife spending time with another dude, wife ceases to spend time with said dude (or at least minimizes how much her husband knows about it). I often see people who are opening up try to minimize pain that's coming up for them when their partner is happy because they've understood that in non-monogamy, you just deal with your jealousy and it's not your partner's responsibility. But what even is jealousy? The deeper I get into my own experience of polyamory and my coaching practice, the less I believe jealousy to be its own emotion. When we say jealousy, we may mean many other things. Emotional experiences commonly mistaken for jealousy:

- Feeling disrespected
- Feeling left out or rejected
- Disappointment
- Being gaslit or mistreated
- Envy
- Fear

Mis-identifying jealousy is a major contributor to miscommunication. If we say, "I'm jealous" when the truth is "I'm disappointed," it can be much harder to properly address any underlying unmet need.

Researchers Richard H. Smith and Sung Hee Kim differentiate jealousy from envy by explaining envy as a desire for something someone else has and jealousy as a fear that someone will take a relationship or part of a relationship that is yours. This is a definition I can get behind as we think about non-monogamy, in part because it limits what we call jealousy and asks us to dig a little deeper to articulate the other aspects of our experience. Emotions researcher Brené Brown explains, "Jealousy doesn't seem to be a singular emotion but rather a cognitive evaluation in response to feeling anger, sadness, and / or fear. In other words, we *think* jealousy in response to how we *feel*."

So, from now on, when you identify jealousy, try looking at it through the lens of the feelings and sensations, and then break it down in terms of the more specific emotions:

- What signals in your body are telling you: "This is jealousy"?
- Are those signals ones you feel in relation to anger, sadness, or fear?
- If you notice anger, sadness, and / or fear, what are those feelings about in this context? Is this something that needs to be addressed? If so, is it better addressed alone or with someone else?

GAME-CHANGERS

One of the things I advocate for, especially early on in opening up, is creating containment around challenging conversations or triggering information. Andi began working with me describing all kinds of hypervigilance – it seemed the more situations he experienced where his long-distance partner was with someone else, the more anxious his body became. He kept thinking he would get used it, but instead what was happening was severely decreased sleep, a feeling of nausea beginning to permeate his everyday, and a lack of concentration at work. As he opened up to me about the details of how they were operating, I found out that they were in communication via text message and voice memo almost constantly, as is common in long-distance dynamics to make up for what might be missing by being in shared physical space. Information about her excursions and activities with other people was permitted to be discussed in this format, and would certainly be discussed via phone or video, whenever they happened to get on a call, seemingly treating "non-monog info" like any other social activity. But, as we've established, when making the transition from monogamy, that which is likely to threaten our sense of secure attachment to our partner is not like other social information.

I helped Andi see that his body was having intense reactions when this info sprang up without warning, and that not having any confines around these emotional bombs was keeping him on edge, particularly because his long-distance partner was far more active in exploring a newfound sense of freedom and sexuality post-divorce. His body was essentially sitting at home waiting for signals of security in their relationship, but learning that it was kind of a fifty-fifty chance of getting safety or getting something threatening it would need to process, in effect, keeping it in self-protective "ready" mode.

When I told him he could request a different, specific structure for communicating information about other lovers, at first, he seemed surprised. What I think is important to understand here is that containment and control are two different things. Creating containment can be setting a weekly time (or whatever frequency works for you) to check in about other relationships and get any information that may be relevant.

The other thing to understand with containment is *what* is it *you* need to know about your partners' other lovers to know what's going on and also maintain your sense of security. There's a trap (I see men fall into more often than women), which is feeling like they need all the details of what has happened with another partner (I mean physically, sexually). This can feel calming once you get the information, but also creates a spike of hypervigilance while waiting for the information, and inevitably will fail to create safety whenever your partner has a sexual experience that *doesn't* reassure you of your place or soothe your insecurities. (Also important to take note of other partners' rights to privacy and what they have consented to sharing.)

The opposite end of this trap is what's commonly referred to as "don't ask, don't tell," (DADT) which is exactly what it sounds like. I see people tend toward this most commonly when they feel their capacity or ability to process is limited. There's a lot of shitting on DADT in the polyam community, which I kind of understand, but I also think is gatekeeping. The arguments against this practice usually center around how it creates secrecy and hiding in a relationship, which can ripple into some pretty serious ruptures in the foundation of the connection. If your partner is falling in love with someone and you have agreed to not know, they have to figure out ways of compartmentalizing that are tiresome for them and keep you at a distance. Or, in the event they're struggling with seeing other people, either not finding anyone they're attracted to or having difficult experiences, it will likely create more shame in them to keep that to themselves. Whereas, if they were allowed to communicate that to you, your reassurance as someone who has dated them would probably go a very long way in them feeling supported.

But instead of just saying "DADT is toxic and doesn't work," I'd rather we get curious. There is a grey area, for sure. *Why* does someone prefer DADT? Are they missing essential resources in order to process hard things? What might the impact of DADT be on their relationships and well-being, and is that actually an appropriate, consensual trade-off for where they are at? What about temporary DADT? Specific circumstances for DADT? There was a point when my c-PTSD got so overwhelming that we closed our relationship until I could get mental health support. I didn't want to be the cause of Itai putting part of his life on hold, and carried guilt about it. At the same time, I understood that we needed to prioritize my mental health in that moment. I've since worked with clients in similar dynamics, whether related to their own mental health, a family member in a health crisis, or someone close to them dying, who have found a temporary DADT agreement to be a good fit while they are tending to something outside the relationship that is overwhelming on its own. For this to work well, there is usually an understanding that they will get caught up on important developments when they have more capacity. There is usually also an understanding that it's not an ideal policy, but it's not an ideal situation. Their partner may need to compartmentalize and source emotional support from other places, but in these scenarios, that is already true.

My point is know your why. Or at least inquire: Why do I feel the need to know X? Why don't I want to know about Z? What impact does knowing or not knowing have on me, and what impact does it have on my partner and our relationship? This inquiry might show you a place of insecurity that is asking for your attention. Or it might show you that you've adopted someone else's rulebook and it doesn't actually fit you and your relationship.

One of the great things about working on communication is there are a lot of hacks that can give us the satisfaction of immediate results. People who communicate about their communication experience greater relationship satisfaction. So just having a conversation about how you communicate is a great step in the right direction. Here are some of my favorites, particularly for non-monogamous contexts:

- *Naming the difference between needing to be heard or witnessed versus a request for problem-solving:* This is at the top of the list because it can so instantly shift everything. In most relationships, there is at least one person who hears their partner in distress, discomfort, complaining and immediately feels responsible for responding with a solution. They may not feel responsible for the implementation of that solution, but their automatic role in the communication will be to look for an answer that will change their partner's negative experience. For many of us, when we're expressing discomfort or challenge, there are times when someone else's solution is welcome and times when we just need to feel seen and heard in our experience. Sometimes we just need to know that they can attune to us and validate our experience. Practice checking in with yourself about this before opening a conversation about something hard; am I looking for problem-solving or am I looking for empathy? Often when we are in the emotional response to something hard, we are in need of empathy before we are capable of appropriately problem-solving. On the flip side, as a receiver, notice if your tendency is to try to fix right away. If your partner tells you they just need to feel heard, how do you respond? If your partner starts talking to you about challenging feelings, first ask them if they know whether they want problem-solving or empathy. Sometimes we don't know but asking will help minimize the kind of conversation where both people leave feeling frustrated and misunderstood.

- *Structuring communication*: Some very basic practices around your communication can help the first three minutes (and more) of that conversation go more smoothly. To start, identify the objective of the conversation; is it to better understand each other's experience, or is it to address something logistical? Then set an amount of time appropriate for the objective. (If you're questioning, err on the shorter side, and if you need more time, schedule another conversation.) Before diving into verbalizing, co-regulate, even if it's just a deep breath together.

- *Take turns reflecting what you've heard:* This is a practice that helps ensure we're hearing what our partner meant to say. Take the conversation in bite-sized chunks. Once one partner has made a point, pause and let the partner who was listening repeat it back using the phrase "I heard…. Do I have that right?"

- *Take responsibility for projections:* When we find ourselves with a particular narrative in our head, fact-check it! Get in the habit of asking the real-life person if the story in your head is true. It can feel scary and vulnerable to say, "My head is telling me you're going to leave me for that other person," or "I have this narrative that you have more fun with other people," but if we don't check whether our narratives are true, they will impact how we're interacting.

Useful phrases to enhance communication:

- "Can we talk?"
- "What I'm hearing is…. Do I have that right?"
- "Do I have your attention?" (Particularly if your partner seems distracted, on their phone, doing other things, ask this before saying something vulnerable.)
- "When (insert) happens, I feel (insert)."
- "Let's take a break."
- "I'm feeling activated / shut down. Can we take some time to regulate and revisit this in X minutes / hours / days?"
- "Thank you for sharing that with me."
- "Thank you for listening."
- "I feel defensive."
- "You communicating X really helped me understand your experience / my impact."

When we start to notice less tension and anxiety, or less time spent fretting over a partner's response, we likely have begun to improve our communication. When we notice that our wants and needs have more definition to them, we have integrated communicating more clearly with ourselves. When we can make specific requests of our partners, express disappointment without blame, and receive what we've asked for with satisfaction, our communication skills are skyrocketing. Like most things in life, great communication takes practice. But also like most things that give us gratification, the satisfying outcomes of good communication make it easier to continue practicing.

9

RE-FRAMING CONFLICT

"The space between disharmony and repair is where intimacy and trust are built."

— COLIN BEDELL

So that was communication, but what happens when communication can't save us from conflict?

Well, first of all, what is conflict? Is conflict the feelings generated as the space between you and your partner grows bigger? Is conflict the miscommunication that grows as your shared quiet grows louder? Is conflict the full-on raging that happens when you both have gotten so confused about your ever-changing agreements that one of you makes a mistake in how to implement them and what ensues is akin to a three-year-old's tantrum?

In simple, concise terms, conflict is the inability or challenge to accept difference. We encounter differences all the time – in opinion, in values, in interpreted meaning. Difference is a defining feature of life, and of human beings in relationships. Where difference poses a challenge to us – whether that means a direct violation of our safety or simply something we struggle to understand – that is where we find conflict.

Remember how there are solvable problems and unsolvable problems in your relationships, and satisfaction depends on choosing the right problems to solve? Conflict itself is an unsolvable problem in that we will never *not* have conflict; all relationships have differences that challenge us. But how we approach conflict may be a problem we get to solve with great satisfaction. What I mean by this is that if we can transform our bracing attitudes about conflict into an embrace of conflict as a natural, important pillar of intimate relating, the satisfaction in our relationships greatly increases. Just to be clear, I don't mean "go fight more." But your central conflict, in particular, can be a case study in how to generate the love you want.

CENTRAL CONFLICT

Every intimate partnership has a central conflict – a difference between the partners that causes friction or tension ... over and over again. The central conflict is a dynamic in which you repeat certain roles that poke at each other's wounds. If you're familiar with attachment theory, you might recognize this in how anxious attachment and avoidant attachment styles play into each other. For example, the workaholic and the anxious fawn will always jab at each other because each of them is looking to get their needs met in different places, and in the process doing exactly what the other wishes they wouldn't. The workaholic is trying to get needs met through professional achievement and wants enough space in relationships to do so. The anxious fawn is trying to get needs met by establishing belonging in relationship and the constant distance while their partner works feels like utter rejection. Another window into central conflict is to think about any archetypes that show up in your relationship, like pleaser, hero, martyr, warrior, worrier, or sage.

Identifying what your role is in your central conflict can help you catch yourself when you are moving away from expressed delight and pleasure toward friction and struggle. We can't always avoid the friction and struggle because relationships have cycles to them, but the knowledge becomes power. It can also be helpful to note if we've assigned positive roles and meaning based on conflict: does this person "prove" their love to me through how we fight?

We will discuss conflict and how to manage it in much greater detail in this chapter. To start, just take a moment to consider your relationship to conflict. Are you someone who sees an opportunity for combat and charges forward? Or are you someone who avoids conflict like the plague? Are there scenarios in which you can stay present to conflict and scenarios in which you simply smooth everything over? If you feel affirmed by conflict, we might want to look for more supportive ways of feeling powerful and cared for. If you avoid conflict, we want to understand why, because non-monogamy will almost undoubtedly present you with situations in which you need to advocate for yourself.

What feelings might you be avoiding by avoiding conflict? And is there anything we can do to soothe *those* feelings so conflict can feel safer?

If you've ever found yourself saying, "I can't believe we're having the same fight again," that is probably a helpful flag in identifying your central conflict. I would then ask if you can identify the roles each of you assume when that conflict gets activated. For example, many relationships have a central conflict that stems from worka-holism. For the person waiting at home while their partner spends another dinner with colleagues, a rejection wound gets activated and they take on a role of acting out to get the attention they need. When the overly worked partner arrives home to a temper tantrum, they take on a "not good enough" role, feeling their partner doesn't appreciate all the effort they put in. Both feel unseen, and rather than finding effective ways to ask their partner to see them, they each take their partner's position as further proof they are not on the same page. The key to unlocking central conflict is you can be hurt and feel unseen, and still meet your partner in the effort to see each other more clearly.

What the central conflict is and which roles you play may change over time, but there are no two humans who fit together in perfect synchronicity (we're not supposed to). Having conflict is not a bad thing, but simply a product of our differences. What you should know is that opening up will exacerbate any unresolved conflicts. So if you haven't figure out how to approach them as a team, it's likely opening up isn't going to "save" your relationship, but amplify whatever tension is there. (The caveat to this specifically relates to sexual dynamics that have gone somewhat dormant. It's not unusual for sleeping with a new person to reignite desire for an existing partner and reinvigorate their sex life. This isn't always the case, but worth noting.)

Rather than guide you to your central conflict, because that could be a whole book unto itself, I want to discuss how non-monogamy often centers two specific wounds – abandonment and rejection. So even if these wounds weren't the source of our conflict before, they very well may be now.

It can be helpful to identify the central conflict of any given relationship so that you can frame it as something you're navigating together. When a problem or conflict arising is framed primarily as one person's responsibility to solve, that problem is much more likely to grow in its detrimental impact. When we can identify what unsolvable conflict is core to our relationship, we can approach it as a realm of mutual learning and make the agreements necessary to improve how we communicate and compromise about it, rather than come with expectations for resolution that leave all parties frustrated and hurt.

RUPTURE HAPPENS

Human relationships involve rupture, or disconnection in varying degrees. Sometimes rupture is a serious violation, and sometimes it's a minor circumstance. We make small mistakes that hurt each other all the time, and not from a place of malice. Often harm happens through simple misunderstanding, or lack of awareness. Sometimes life circumstances mean we're simply not as available or attentive as our partner needs. But accepting that rupture will happen, and we will experience hurt is the strongest foundation from which to approach conflict.

Not all rupture is conflict, but all conflict is rupture. One form of rupture is simply increased time apart or perceived distance or disconnection from a close relationship. I often tell clients that early non-monogamy is a lot like building new muscle in the body; the same way muscle fibers build up through cycles of tearing and repairing, we undergo more ruptures than usual through the process of opening up, and the strength of the relationship is developed from the processes of repairing those ruptures.

However, if we're not particularly skilled at repairing

ruptures (i.e., coming back to our sense of connectedness), the stress of undergoing it more and in new ways can exacerbate other ruptures and turn into full-blown fighting.

REPAIR

If we think of rupture as a break in connection, then one of the most accessible ways to facilitate repair is to consciously attune to one of our small-but-mighty moments. If we can still access the sweet, juicy goodness of the tiny connective gestures, it's easy to come back from feeling apart. This is where return rituals shine. If you have just spent the night with a different partner and you are returning home, you are entering a space where some repair is necessary. This is not to say you have done anything wrong, but simply that a gap has been created between you and the partner you're returning to, and that gap needs some tending to. Identifying rituals that tend to the gap can help us embody this acceptance of rupture and repair, and can keep us from slipping into the sense of shame or guilt that comes with misinterpreting rupture as a harmful thing we should be "fixing."

My client, Julie, was describing to me a dynamic in which every time she returned home to her nesting partner from spending the night with her boyfriend, conflict would ensue. The pattern went something along the lines of: return home, go back to normal routines, feel like her partner was ignoring her or being very short, hours later start to fight about household chores and the distribution of labor. The way she explained it, he wasn't dating anyone else and didn't really want to put effort into dating anyone else, but she wasn't convinced that imbalance was actually OK. Whenever she returned home from her boyfriend's she felt guilty and didn't want to "rub it in his face" that she was just with someone else, so she would do her best to go right to doing something else or steer the conversation away from where she had just been.

What she thought was being considerate was actually making the rupture more intense by failing to acknowledge it. The space between them would expand, with her partner living in the narrative that she didn't care to reconnect with him and her living in the narrative that he was mad at her for having another relationship. We created a ritual for them that addressed the repair by calling upon some of their known shared pleasure. Whenever Julie came home from that point on, she would bring him a croissant from his favorite bakery, and they would spend six to ten minutes cuddling and talking to reconnect (six minutes of physical contact is also very supportive of a stronger sexual connection). She would be sure to start the interaction with "I missed you" so that her absence and their separation were acknowledged. Sure enough, the first time they implemented their return ritual, there was no fight about the dishes.

ANATOMY OF FORGIVENESS

But what happens when you need to repair something that has involved a violation? What happens if your agreements about safer sex practices are broken, or your partner wasn't transparent about how much they've been seeing their new lover? Well, that requires forgiveness. Forgiveness is a choice. It's not something that just happens. If we think it has "just happened" that we've moved on, we are likely holding an imprint of the violation with us. Research says that holding a grudge increases cortisol, so let's not do that if we can help it. True forgiveness after a violation of trust requires repair of some kind. Sometimes all it takes is acknowledgment, but there has to be something.

General flow looks like: rupture, acknowledgment, decision to forgive, accountability, amends, adaptation. The keys to accountability are acknowledgment of one's role, ownership of impact, and demonstration of change that minimizes the risk of repeating the violation. (That change can be behavior, but also understanding. Sometimes demonstrating a change in understanding how the circumstance was created is enough to rebuild the trust).

When we make the decision to forgive in an ongoing, intimate relationship, we are also making the decision to look at the bigger picture. True forgiveness requires some level of self-awareness to understand what we might need from the other person in order to move forward with trust. Without articulating our needs, or looking at how all parties contributed to the violation, we may remain gripping onto the hurt. In the example of a partner not being transparent about their time with a new lover, we might first want to find out if the agreement wasn't clear. If the agreement *was* clear, do we make a choice to just let it go? Or do we need to understand our partner's reason for doing what they did? Is it enough for us simply to listen to their experience and empathize with the fact that they were afraid to tell us about their growing feelings for someone else? For some of us, sure. And for some of us, it will be easier to trust that this mistake won't be repeated if we figure out a way to address it collaboratively. That might mean requesting a weekly check-in about other partners so things can't accumulate again.

It's also important that we practice forgiving ourselves. If we beat ourselves up over ways we've been unapproachable or ruptures that have hurt our partners, it can have the impact of creating aversion around similar situations

in the future. When we're talking about the very conditions of non-monogamy contributing to the rupture, it
won't work for you to sacrifice the dating and sex life you
want because you can't forgive yourself for forgetting to
check in that one time, or coming home later than you
agreed, or getting an STI because the agreements about
safer sex hadn't been fully developed yet. We have to be
able to forgive ourselves in order to keep showing up in
more fully expressed ways.

Furthermore, being too hard on ourselves is often a
self-protection mechanism that actually impedes intimacy.
One of the conflicts in my nesting partnership revolves
around my time blindness. More than once, I have been
very late coming home from a date or have pushed the
agreed upon time right up to the edge. Once I was having
drinks on a first date, got hungry, and lost track of time
ordering food to the point where I came home almost two
hours later from what I had guessed would be a ninety-
minute meet-up. Rather than allow space for my partner to
express his feelings, the guilt and shame that came with
beating myself up took up all the air in the room. By the
time I pulled into the driveway I was crying, visibly more
upset than he, and needing to be consoled and calmed to a
certain degree. We have to be able to hold space for our
own mistakes if we want our partners to have the space to
express themselves to us.

HOW WE HAVE DONE CONFLICT

Most of us learned conflict as something scary, or as a
means of compensating for other areas of pain in our life.
Some families express connection and care through fighting, and others avoid confrontation at all costs. Very few of
us grew up with helpful models of conflict resolution in

our family contexts, so when it comes to conflict in our adult intimacy, naturally we have a lot of stuff to unpack.

Even if we're equipped with great communication skills, most of us still have an adverse reaction to conflict in our partnerships. It's not enjoyable, and it usually makes us feel disconnected, misunderstood, angry, sad, or some combination of all of the above. Sometimes our deepest wounds and self-protection patterns come up when we are feeling safe enough to work through them, but more often, our deepest vulnerabilities are triggered by conflict. The difference at the core of conflict can be interpreted subconsciously as a threat to our belonging, which brings us right back to the earlier chapters. Now hear me out: what if it's not that conflict with our partner that makes us feel those things, but rather it reveals that we are already experiencing those things?

How many of us have had the experience of looking around after an hour of arguing and thinking, "I don't even know what we're talking about anymore or how we got here?" Probably everyone reading this book. Well, how you got there is probably due to the fact that there's a lot of conflict already occurring, but not being communicated clearly. If we adopt the understanding of conflict as a challenge that arises from difference, it's possible that the feelings you're struggling with on your own are conflict in and of themselves, whether or not you verbalize them to your partner. When that internal experience of conflict builds up and we finally have an external, verbalized argument (i.e., express conflict in the shared space of the relationship), it's hard for us to internally separate the internal and external sources of our experience of conflict. So suddenly the argument about who forgot to take out the trash is touching on that time you forgot to keep the agreement of scheduling a date with your primary partner every time you do an overnight with someone else.

Now, I'm not saying that every little annoyance or struggle needs to be verbally communicated to your partner in order to have a healthy relationship with conflict. But I am saying that conflict is happening, whether or not it gets your shared, direct, verbal communication. I'm also saying that if we can accept this as an unsolvable problem, how we engage in conflict changes drastically. Our goal is not to eradicate conflict from our relationships, but to learn how to embrace it as a tool for deepening intimacy.

CONFLICT IS GENERATIVE

In the same way that boundaries are important for a supportive partnership, conflict is a necessary component of ongoing intimacy. At their core, both of these concepts honor the fact of our maintained difference. We cannot become the same person as any of our partners, nor should we. We cannot know every single thing about our partners, nor should we. Instead, it is the paradox of both being attracted to what we know about someone and the mystery of getting to learn more about them that sustains our relationship with them.

When conflict happens, it shows us our differences. When we communicate our differences to each other, we are gifting each other the opportunity to clarify how we'd like to operate in a relationship. Learning more about our differences gets to be a chance to care for each other better, more deeply, more effectively.

How many of us have also had the experience of overcoming a major hurdle in a relationship and feeling like the partnership was stronger because of it? That's the generative quality of conflict that we navigate with vulnerability and teamwork.

In early polyamory, conflict often shows up as a result of misaligned expectations, unclear agreements, and being forced to confront your own assumptions about your partner. How your partner operated in certain situations under monogamy gave you a particular view of them that might not be true of their desires or behavior in non-monogamy. Remember, through the process of opening up, you're meeting new parts of them, but also new parts of yourself, and the same is true of your partner's experience. With so much newness, it would be wild to not also encounter challenging differences.

I frame conflict as part of intimacy because in revealing all these differences, we are showing each other vulnerable parts of ourselves. Perhaps even the most vulnerable parts of ourselves, because it is in conflict that our wounds and self-protection patterns are most easily activated.

OBSTACLES TO GENERATIVE CONFLICT

People-Pleasing and Fawning

These are all attempts to avoid conflict by performing sameness instead of difference. When we try to make others happy and it's not in aligned action to our own desire, it adds deception to existing conflict. It might smooth things over in the moment, but ultimately it compounds the conflict.

Attachment to Role of Peacekeeper

Particularly if we grew up amidst conflict or chaos, many of us learn to establish safety or belonging in our younger years by taking on the role of peacekeeper. We become diligent at understanding others' points of view and empathizing in such a way as to diffuse tension. This survival mechanism is wise but stands in the way of asking our partner to meet us where we are. It means we are used to going to them.

Defensiveness

Generating intimacy relies on all parties' capacities to take responsibility for their own actions, thoughts, and contributions to a dynamic, whether or not the result is aligned with their intention. Defensiveness stands in the way of being able to integrate new information or perspectives. It is likely also a signal you're having some fight or flight response, so consider your regulation tools.

Porous Boundaries / Taking Too Much Responsibility

When we take all the responsibility for creating a conflict or solving a problem, we rob our partner of the opportunity to voice their feelings about it, and also to collaborate with us in creating solutions. Not only is it not your responsibility to have all the answers figured out before you open up a dialogue, doing so actually excludes your partner from the problem-solving process, which can be another conflict-contributor.

This is an expression of porous boundaries because it is an inaccurate assessment of what's my responsibility versus what is your responsibility. Or rather, there's no line between where my responsibility ends and yours begins. In a conflict where all parties have right-fit boundaries in place, each person takes ownership of their own role, but respects that each person has a role. One person's responsibility has to be clearly defined (to have a boundary or an end) in order for another person to be able to claim theirs.

TIPS FOR IMPROVING GENERATIVE CONFLICT

Be with Yourself First

If you are feeling the tension rising and a fight building, it can be immensely beneficial to take the time to assess your own position in it and do your best to separate your feelings from facts. This becomes harder to do when we are actively *in* an argument or heated discussion.

Some self-inquiry prompts I recommend when conflict is bubbling:

- Are any needs of mine not being met? Not just specific to the conflict, but in general. If I'm hungry or feeling socially isolated, for example, that will elevate my sense of threat. If any of those needs can be met before addressing the conflict, do that.
- What am I feeling? What are the thoughts associated with this state? Have I felt this way before? If yes, is that situation resolved?
- If I could ask for anything at all (and know it would be granted to fix this), what would I ask for? Does the answer I came up with here feel

like it is actually about the person in front of me, or about another situation in my life?

Set Intentions and Time Limits

When there is conflict to address, get clear on the shared objective of the particular conversation you're having. Does someone need to be heard? Is there a logistical issue to figure out?

If you often find yourself in fights going, "I don't even know what we're talking about," start by making a list (together) of what you think the pieces are that need to be addressed. When you look at that list, you might realize you need to schedule separate conversations for each part.

Not mentioned in the ABCs of Trauma Resolution, but containment is a very important skill in trauma work. This is the relational application of containment.

Teamwork

Start with the question for each other: is there an easy way to shift the framing from me versus you to us versus the problem? Sometimes all it takes is a perspective shift. If we have both made mistakes recently due to being depleted or over-scheduled, how can we support each other to get enough rest?

Map Your Compromises

Often when we compromise or sacrifice, our memory formation focuses on what we've given up. Tracking where you and your partner have both made accommodations will help reinforce the feeling that this is actually a team effort, acting as a buffer against resentment.

Getting Comfortable with Rage

I can't recall a single woman I've worked with who felt comfortable accessing her anger at the beginning of our work. Anger is there to tell you a boundary has been crossed. Anger is the natural emotional activation that comes with boundary violation. But where we have manipulated our nervous systems to befriend or fawn, we have distanced ourselves from a healthy anger response. Intimacy involves the full spectrum of human emotion, including anger.

Consider working with a professional for this one. We certainly can tap into supportive, appropriate anger on our own, and if it's been suppressed for a while, you may stir up a lot of psyche material at once. One of the (many) reasons it's useful to get professional support with these kinds of processes is that if it's old, unprocessed anger coming up, you might misdirect it toward your partner. A trained professional can act as a buffer so that those misdirected emotions don't inflict unnecessary harm on your partnership.

That said, not everyone has access to a right-fit coach or therapist, and there are some very effective ways to work with anger on your own. Often my clients who have a hard time feeling anger are actually misidentifying it. They'll show up in sessions saying they're frustrated, anxious, depleted. Begin by asking yourself if there might be something to be angry about in what you're experiencing, even if that emotion isn't front and center for you. If we think of anger as a healthy response to violation we might consider if any boundaries are being crossed (like over-working your body).

A somatic practice I sometimes do with clients is to actually throw a tantrum. Honestly, what works for kids works for grown-ups; there is an incredible wisdom in the physical expression of a three-year-old. Anger or rage activate our body's responses, and screaming, kicking, flailing, and wailing work wonders for discharging that activation from the body. The next time you have even a tiny little glimmer of anger, take it directly to the nearest bed or couch and have a pillow fight with yourself. You can punch the mattress. You can bury your face and scream into the pillow. You can lie on your back and kick and punch the air until you are worn out. This may sound ridiculous, but not only does this exercise help us move anger through, it also helps soothe the fear that we won't be able to contain the anger once we tap into it (a common fear for many people I work with). If you tantrum until you are tired, you will most likely find the activation is lessened, your chest a little broader, your breath a little deeper, etc.

Resource with Pleasure Practices

Before diving into potential tension, is there something you can do together to connect?

If you know you're going into a conversation about something that has *not* been going well, begin by communicating two to three things that *have* been going well. This reminds you both of the pleasure you experience with each other, and helps support your social engagement system.

After experiencing disconnection or tension, what pleasure can bring you back together? Use this pleasure as a reminder of where and how you *do* connect. This helps contextualize the tension; it is only one aspect of many in your relationship.

In my nesting partnership, it is the rupture resulting from travel that tends to stir up conflict. The distance between us easily bleeds from geographical into emotional, and it can be particularly hard to address conflict from a distance, so inevitably there is residue upon arriving home. Does that mean we come in swinging as soon as we are reunited? No, it means we get in our animal bodies first. We find playfulness and reconnection through touch, breathing together, or even sometimes getting on the floor and pretend wrestling.

Observe the Body in Conflict

When you're communicating conflict with your partner, where is the edge of the window of tolerance? This can be tricky to teach ourselves to identify, but the shortcut is noticing a combination of the following: ability to both listen to someone else and notice your extremities, an internal "speeding up" of energy but also thoughts, losing capacity for eye contact, lump in throat, tightness in chest, impulse to run away / move body, gripping hands / fists / arms, impulse to change your body language (notice when the impulse is to puff up and out versus when the impulse is to curl in or slouch). Have you already passed it by the time you're communicating with them? If so, your work is to learn to communicate earlier.

Make Your Partner a "Trigger Manual"

Much of conflict gets escalated beyond useful communication because we enter a process of co-triggering. A trigger manual can help us help each other de-escalate, and it can also be a great intimacy-builder.

Here are some examples:

- "When Pixie is in *hyper-* response it might look like: raising voice and speeding up, tension and heat in her body and face, interrupting, blaming, losing her appetite, or getting nauseous. Things that help: drinking water, going for a run or walk, ecstatic dance in the living room, yelling into a pillow, orgasm, bear hugs and breathing together."

- "When Bobbi is in *hypo-* it might look like rejecting attempts for connection, having a hard time figuring out what to say / not having anything to say, over-responsibility or "it's all my fault." Things that help: loving words from partner, massage, gentle yoga, flogging and spanking, five-senses orienting practice."

Go to Bed Mad

I mean take breaks. Only come back to the conflict when you've returned to the window of tolerance. While on a break, resource yourself with your own pleasure.

Regularly Schedule Hard Conversations

You know how "We need to talk" carries the weight of "Oh shit, something's about to go down?" but usually by the time someone is saying, "We need to talk," everyone involved already knows what the conversation is about? We actually always have some degree of experiencing our differences. When we normalize this, it helps reprogram some of the fear and bracing we experience around conflict in general.

Take the *Right Amount* of Responsibility

In a dynamic, nothing is ever entirely one person's fault or doing. (Caveat: I'm not talking about abuse here.) Even if you have a bone to pick with your partner, can you also listen to their experience and reflect upon how you might have contributed to the conflict? Can you see where maybe they're blaming you for *more* than what you are responsible for, but still see the parts that are true?

Reflect and Integrate What You've Learned

The information that comes from generative conflict can help you update all the guidelines of your relationship to be a better fit. Whenever you've reached some resolution in the conflict, make sure you're clear on any changes in your shared agreements.

Generative conflict deepens intimacy by showing us new parts of our partners and ourselves. Coming out of conflict, ask yourself what you've learned about yourself and your partner. How does this information enable you to both love and receive love better than before? Is there any new information about what helps prevent / minimize this particular conflict? Any new information about what helps us reconnect after conflict?

Is there anything about the outcome of this conflict that might impact other partners / dates / pals in your life? What communication do you need to have outside of this relationship?

Come Back Together

Conflict does damage when it keeps us apart. It is a life-changing skill to practice togetherness in the face of conflict. When you've reached a compromise, or are just taking a pause, can you find a way of reconnecting that reminds you both of your shared expressed delight? You might still also be angry, or frustrated, or tired, but can you *also* experience affection or laughter or joy alongside it? Trying to do so will help the conflict stay contained and help you remember it is only one aspect of your partnership.

RE-THINKING COLLABORATION

"True belonging doesn't require you to change who you are; it requires you to be who you are."

— BRENÉ BROWN

P artnerships are laboratories of collaboration. Understanding the terms of the experiment is essential for gauging how it's going. What's the hypothesis? What are the methods? How are you analyzing the results? What safety measures do you need in order to avoid explosions in the lab? What unexpected creation gets to spring forth from your experiment and astound the world with its magic?

Our partners' triggers and perceptions are not our responsibility, exactly. But the whole notion of interdependence prompts us to look at how we can collaborate to create a relationship context that helps minimize triggers and / or provides the necessary support for alchemizing them. In this way, intimacy can be profoundly healing for those of us with attachment wounds. Really, interdependence isn't a notion so much as a fact; we are all interdependent living on this planet together. To what extent we strive to live congruently with that fact is a different question.

My client, Becks, came to session with an activation around a partner interaction they'd had recently. They were in the ambivalent place of "I know my old relationship trauma is getting activated and I'm having a hard time trusting my judgment. Part of me wants to just end it." I asked them what the agreements of the relationship were, and they responded that there were intentions, not agreements. And in the time since they had set those intentions, their partner had escalated three other relationships, notably impacting the dynamic between the two of them. When I asked what they desired as the outcome of the current conundrum (related to scheduling and travel to see one of his other partners), the response was something like, "Well, I'm waiting to see what his decision is with the travel piece, and then I'll know more about what makes sense for me."

I realized they were confused in part because they were trying to make an assessment without a metric – how do we know if something is serving us if we haven't defined how to measure it? Just because non-monogamy centers autonomy and asks us to disentangle from defaults in relationships does not mean we just sit back and see how things unfold (unless that is, truly, your pleasurable way of doing relationships). We can save ourselves a lot of energy, analysis, and grief if we're willing to ask for the structure that responds to our wants and needs, regardless of how "serious" a relationship is.

Chances are, if you grew up as a woman in our dominant culture, you weren't really taught to approach relationships as a collaboration. It's more likely that you were conditioned from a young age to care more about what boys thought of you than whether or not you actually liked them. So forgive me if it sounds obvious, but I'm taking your cultural context into consideration when I say that relationships should be approached as a collaboration, a teamwork experience. Where your opening up process has gone awry, you have probably lost some of your sense of teamwork, whether that's due to the unfortunate pitfall that is individualism or just traversing unexpected hurdles without instructions on *how* to approach them as a team.

Hopefully at this point you have some clarity about what was making you feel unclear before. Now comes the step where we bring it all together in order for you to live into what you really want out of non-monogamy. If you approach every connection / partnership / intimate relationship / fling / casual hookup / whatever you prefer to call it in *your* non-monogamy as a collaboration, what is it that you need for those collaborations to be in alignment for you?

In general, collaboration requires different but complementary characteristics and / or skills. Collaboration tends to focus on a specific project or task, which means there is definition to the roles and responsibilities. Good collaborators adjust with each other as they go, which requires some give and take, as well as communication.

Really, wildly successful collaborations have clear contracts in addition to intuitive chemistry. Now, for most people it doesn't scream "sexy" to talk contracts, but having a detailed understanding of what's involved in a collaboration creates the circumstances for creative expression and connection to flourish. Without community guiding us to these kinds of practices and conversations, many early non-monogamists skip over the full negotiation of their relationship guidelines. But this is where we are no longer relying on the structure of monogamy for our sense of security, so we must dive into greater detail to understand the foundational components of a mutually supportive relationship, so that we have a shared framework for what it is we're communicating about.

BRADS: GUIDELINES FOR INTIMATE COLLABORATION

The elements of a relationship contract are boundaries, rules / restrictions, agreements, and support. In my version of this I also include dreams, or dream scenario. This is because I believe it helps us to open up new relational possibilities to be able to name our fantasies. Setting the tone that we are welcome to share what we want can also grant us more permission to be where we are now. Communicating the dream to a partner can help us to hold it in mind and can ultimately make it more attainable to have their support / involvement.

On the flip side, expectations do come into play, and might require a little bit of reality checking the other components. Before we can properly negotiate agreements and requests that will actually serve us, we must take stock of where we currently are, and what expectations we might need to adjust accordingly. For example, if I am having panic attacks every time my partner goes on a date with his other partner, it's probably not realistic for me to expect that next time he goes on a date, I will be full of compersion.

So let's just lay out each of these elements of the acronym BRADS:

- *Boundaries* – limits you maintain for yourself. For example, if you have a boundary that you won't date people with more than a ten-year age difference, it is up to you to check people's age before you begin dating them. Sounds like: "I will…"
- *Rules / restrictions* – code of conduct or behavior we ask of our partner, usually to contain our own triggering, and usually enforced by threat of punishment or consequence. This gets a bad rap in the non-monogamy world because the whole idea is relational freedom, and rules usually sound like imposing our own stuff on someone else. They challenge some understandings of consent because there is a certain air of coercion involved in making a rule for someone else (unless, of course, it's part of a consensual kink dynamic). Generally, not a great idea in intimate partnership (outside of kink) because our sense of autonomy is diminished when we feel we have no choice in a situation. *However,* I think they are worth mentioning in the early opening of existing relationships simply for the purpose of not overloading the relationship and creating irreparable harm from taking on too many partners or too much processing in a short period of time. Sounds like: "You can't…"
- *Agreements* – codes of conduct for behavior consensually negotiated by both collaborators. Usually these are guidelines that refer to both parties' behaviors and are understood as mutually supportive of each other 's pleasure and growth, as well as the central mission. If not adhering to the same behavior, *usually* there will

be a balancing agreement. Requires trust. Sounds like: "We will…"

- *Dream scenarios* – your ideal scenario for this connection. Does this feel long-term or short-term? What role is this person playing for you? How would you like things to operate when you're not together? Sharing dream scenarios regularly can help our communication and intimacy by bringing in hopefulness and creativity where sometimes we might feel overly technical or emotionally flooded. This can also be a way of figuring out the right time to revisit your relationship contract. Dream scenarios are often overlooked in our discussions of communication, but they are beautiful inquiries for ensuring our agreements are aligned with each other and for deepening our understanding of our partners. Sounds like: "I would love…"

- *Support:* contempt and criticism are both on the list of top predictors of divorce. And when they seep into our relationships, usually they are a misguided attempt at communicating a desire. If we can learn to identify the requests beneath the criticisms, we will save ourselves a lot of struggle. For example, if I feel inclined to tell my partner, "You're a workaholic," am I communicating that out of concern for them, or because I am actually desiring more of their time and attention? Identifying a request and communicating it, we may be met with a no, but then we can look into getting that request met in a different way rather than having it fester into contempt. Sounds like: "I'd like to request…" or

"I have a need / desire for... Can you help me fulfill it?"

Do you know what your existing relationship agreements are? For example, when my partner and I started this whole thing, we made an agreement very early on that we would inform other people about our relationship before sleeping with them. To both of us, that felt like the ethical approach to consent around an open relationship. We also made an agreement to use condoms in all sexual encounters. Take a few moments before we move on and write down a list of your existing relationship agreements.

OK, done? Now look at that list again and make note of anything on it that hasn't been explicitly discussed and agreed upon with your partner. If they have not explicitly confirmed their participation in that agreement, it is actually an expectation. An expectation is something that is solely yours, and can influence how we feel about our partners' conduct, without them necessarily knowing. Are there any expectations on your list?

Now, if I ask you to think of this relationship as a creative endeavor, what is it you want to create? Adventure? Growth? What from previous chapters and holistic pleasure informs your vision? Are there any agreements that would help you feel safer and more supported in this collaboration that are not already on your list?

The thing that gets talked about less in relationship self-help is, "How do you want to be as a partner?" When we're stepping into this work looking to repair some rupture, most of our attention is on how to get our partner to see and hear us differently, how to get our needs met, etc. But an essential part of relationship is the experience of expressing our love and affection for our beloveds. It can also be a beautiful way to tap into the sense of collaboration for us to hear from each other not just, "Here's how to love me better" but also, "Here's how I love to express my love for you." So how do you want to be as a partner? What gestures, behaviors, roles bring you the most pleasure as a partner loving on your partner? Are they able to receive that from you? Can you affirm and receive your partner's preferred expressions of love toward you?

COLLABORATION AS CONSENT

You may be thinking to yourself, "I'm not totally rethinking here; I already saw partnerships as collaborations." And if that's you, great, I'm happy to hear that. The reason I'm harping on it is that it requires conscious effort to collaborate in a way that doesn't reinforce the systems that shaped us. We all take on roles in different areas and relationships, and framing partnership as a collaborative process is an effort to garner more consensual relationship to our roles.

Collaborating on Your Right-Fit Non-Monogamy

Your right-fit non-monogamy is whatever works for where you're currently at. You can know deep within your bones that you want to move toward a non-hierarchical, kitchen table polyamory structure, but also need to first address that you and your partner both get destabilized seeing each other with someone else. It's OK to have agreements in place that are problematic but allow you to work toward the dream scenario step by step.

For this reason (and many others) BRADS, ideally, should be reviewed periodically and should touch not only on how you conduct yourselves inside of the partnership, but what is needed outside the space of togetherness for you to be well resourced to be the partner you want to be, and be able to receive the partnership you desire.

Make your contracts with holistic pleasure in mind, setting yourselves up to resourcing yourself and your relationships with the vitality of orienting to what is good. What questions do you need to consider for you to feel secure and nourished as you and your partner take these courageous steps both toward other people and deeper into your intimacy?

- Agreements for self-care
- Agreements around hierarchy
- Agreements about how to communicate
- Agreements about shared resources

BRADS also become a useful tool in keeping us in a collaborative state while we address more acutely stressful situations. At exactly the moment where negotiation might grow contemptuous, grabbing a sheet of paper and saying, "Let's look at our BRADS for this sex party / romantic trip with another partner / high stress period / whatever life may be throwing at you," can help create clear understanding from a felt sense of togetherness, as opposed to descending into the feelings of abandonment or rejection that might try to hijack the narrative. When you're choosing to face new, exciting, expansive, but also potentially deeply challenging and painful experiences *together*, collaboration will help move you from triggered to doable, to dripping in pleasure.

PLEASURE LIBERATION (A.K.A. THE POLYAMOROUS AGENDA)

"The lifestyle has liberated me. I'm the best version of myself, a version I didn't even think was possible before."

— PLEASURE COACHING CLIENT

Cheers to you, dear reader! You made your way through a plethora of information about the infinite challenges we face as part of being human. How are you doing with all that? My dream for you is that you feel inspired, hopeful, and equipped with more tools than you had at the start of this book. My not-so-secret ulterior motive is something akin to the gay agenda, but polyamory. Just kidding ... kind of. No, but really, part of me does want to awaken everyone's alignment to the practice of non-monogamy because polyamorous people do still face significant hurdles in this society. And I do believe those hurdles work in a bidirectional way, the same way the hurdles of biphobia do. Where we experience fluidity in our sexuality, it will require significant forces for us to realize we are anything other than the dominant culture's prescription for us. If we are not nurtured to explore the range of our desire, we will default to what keeps us more socially safe. I believe the same is true of our relational orientation and love style. Without the context that supports and encourages us to explore our non-monogamous drive, it is hard to imagine ourselves fully in it.

Humans are creatures of habit. I know that most of you reading this book won't implement the changes it offers you. That's not a judgment or a criticism – it's just what I know to be true about humans. We stay in our painful habits because they have served us in some way. Fear will tell you this particular process of liberation sounds scary, isolating even. It will whisper, "It's not worth it. Don't risk the loss."

Lacking community and role models is one of the major reasons why some people stay stuck where they are in opening up, or decide it's just not worth it and throw in the towel. It can be hard to tell what our options are or what we truly desire beyond what we have known. It can be even harder to understand how to get from where we are now to where we think we might want to be if we don't have real relationships in our lives to model the steps. And for those who stick with it, but feel isolated in terms of non-monogamous community, the mis-attuned comments from friends and / or the fear of revealing themselves to family can really take a toll. Imagine laying your most vulnerable relationship stuff on the table to your best friend, and where you're looking for empathy you repeatedly receive, "I don't know how you do it."

When friends and family aren't the answer, it's not uncommon to turn to professional help. And while competency for supporting non-monogamous people is certainly expanding with the demand, finding "right-fit" support is often still an uphill battle. The first therapist I saw as I was opening up often asked me, "And how could this be different if you were monogamous?" I felt like she was constantly trying to lead the black sheep back to the herd against its will. Another therapist I saw a couple years later claimed to be LGBTQ-affirming and versed in polyamory, but then advised me that if I wanted more sexual experience with women, I should remove my relational orientation from my Tinder profile. Lesbians wouldn't respond well to seeing "non-monogamous" on my dating profile, he said.

I understand if, even with all the right tools, you still have questions about your own path. I respect whatever purpose staying in the anxiety and overwhelm may serve for you. There is safety, there is belonging in the known discomfort, even if we hate it. Sometimes we're just not ready to do the work because we're afraid of what we'll find. Our psyches will spin all kinds of webs and take us into all the twisty-turny nooks and crannies trying to avoid loss or major disruption of how we understand ourselves. I'm not here to convince you to create change before you're ready. I know better than that; you have to be the one to choose.

A while back, Jessica Daylover was coaching me, and as she honed in on the unsolvable problem in my primary partnership, and its very evident misalignment to my needs, I told her I simply wasn't ready to deal with that as truth. Yes, me not being domestically partnered to a touring musician was the conclusion that made the most sense, but I was not equipped to face that loss in my life if I had any choice in it. Solving that problem would have created a whole slew of other problems that I was exercising my agency *not* to choose. "Fair enough," she said. "I applaud your self-awareness."

Funnily enough, articulating this to her, allowing myself to be honest and vulnerable about it, finally clicked something into place for me where I had been struggling for years; I realized that much of the conflict I'd been engaging with was maintaining the script around this unsolvable problem. I was not looking at the problems that I *could* solve because all of my focus was on protecting myself from what would happen if the unsolvable problem forced me to leave. I realized this was an exercise in my own agency, just one that was causing me more pain than pleasure. Making some subtle changes in how I exercised that agency made all the difference in the world. The irony is that it empowered me to face the risk of losing my partner, and in turn, that made our relationship unbreakable.

And I'll just throw it on the table, it may be that you are with the wrong-fit partner to feel nurtured and secure in your polyamory....

The fear of our own sexuality is a little bit different in that there's internalized homophobia or biphobia we will have to confront should the unraveling of compulsory monogamy begin to pull on the thread of compulsory heterosexuality. Again, I invite us back to trusting the body. It knows things about your safety, your self-expression, your connection to others that the mind will never know. If it's not ready to pull on that thread, I say trust it. Of course, I want you to be your most expansive, fulfilled, fully-expressed self. But if you honor the no, once the yes is ready, it will be so much clearer and stronger because it will be coming from a place of full self-consent.

Additionally, the level of discomfort or dysregulation you consent to is up to you. Sometimes that means realizing the benefit isn't worth the cost to you at this time, and that's OK. If you feel a real attraction to a non-monogamous structure, but are too overwhelmed and triggered when you step toward it, you may want to do some trauma work first.

However, I invite you to consider your positive affect tolerance. Or, in simpler terms, your capacity for pleasure. The same way we have a limit to how much stress our bodies can properly digest, we have a limit to how much goodness we can deal with. Until you make the choice to work on your capacity for pleasure, your baseline of pain won't really change.

Your positive affect tolerance is directly informed by your position in pleasure oppression. And while I respect your personal timeline for healing, I also believe none of us is free without each other's liberation. Whenever you're ready, your personal pleasure renaissance won't just be about you. Your choice to heal, to receive more aligned support, to claim what you want without shame or restriction, to communicate more clearly and conflict more generatively, to engage with your pleasure as your guiding force will also liberate those around you.

SEX, DRUGS, AND INTIMACY

I was running late to meet some people for a pre-sex party drink, and of course had forgotten that parking was a thing. As I circled West Hollywood, my feelings of urgency scanning for empty spaces along the curb were momentarily replaced by a flutter of excitement when I remembered that I would finally meet Ava that night. Ava is a friend of a friend from the community Itai and I have been fostering.

The only time I'd really spoken with Ava was a phone call several weeks before. Not much to go off, but we had recognized ourselves in one another instantly. Quite simply, we spoke each other's language. I was starting to notice that claiming what I truly wanted in all the different realms of my life brought me new relationships that I was actually excited about. (Remember my tendency to date whoever happened to be there in the beginning?)

Itai wasn't with me that night, owning his desire for solo creative time in the music studio while I pursued mine for excitement and social connection. That night I was also meeting up with another couple I'd become close to. When Ava arrived with her partner, Taylor, I was giddy. It was the first sex party Taylor was attending. I don't care how practiced you are at polyamory, when you find your-self in a new, socially vulnerable situation, feelings of awkwardness trepidation or anxiety will always show up at least for a moment. Thankfully in this instance, that moment of feeling out of sync passed very quickly. In an effort to put Taylor more at ease, we all began sharing tales of what to expect. After the waitress had delivered a round of drinks and we had found our way to a comfortable rhythm of conversation, the topic turned toward the night ahead.

We went around the table describing our desires and intentions for that particular evening. The exercise grounded me; a potent reminder that everyone is bringing a unique want, and often that comes with a universal inse-curity. Where I may have once found my head spinning, trying to think my way out of the discomfort of being a fifth wheel in a heightened setting, I felt safe. I was happy to be with two people who already meant so much to me, and excited to explore with these two people who were down to be open with complete strangers on their way to a sex party.

My mind periodically drifted to Itai. I simultaneously missed him, was grateful to feel so secure entering this setting without him, and looking forward to returning home to him … but not just yet.

We paid the bill at the bar just in time to get inside the venue before they closed the doors. As we all oriented ourselves to the layout of people in lingerie and various stations for all kinds of exploration, I marveled at having so many experiences and relationships in my life that I couldn't quite categorize by my old vocabulary. My rela-tional landscape seemed to be ever-evolving in the direction of just "connection." Just after I found myself sharing a pair of fluffy pink handcuffs with a bisexual British guy who was visiting L.A. from San Francisco, I found myself getting flogged by the guy he was with. Ava's face suddenly appeared in front of mine while I was on all fours on the flogging table. "May I kiss you?" she asked. "How did you know that's exactly what I wanted?" I answered.

While I didn't have sex that night, I did nurture various intimacies in ways I couldn't have dreamed of before non-monogamy. And as I drove out of West Hollywood around 2:00 a.m., I marveled at how present I'd been in my body all night, available to new people and experiences as they unfolded. More than that, I marveled at how all the work I'd put into healing through non-monogamy had brought Itai and I to a place where I wasn't overly concerned about him or our relationship. I pursued my own pleasure, knowing that was reciprocated and that we had the skills under our belts to continue to transform new challenges into deeper intimacy in the coming chapters of our lives.

For my birthday a few weeks later, Itai and I turned off our phones and had an LSD date. Whenever we do LSD dates, we ritualize it with an intention-setting and a trip-closing. I keep all the notes from the trip closings in the same small, black notebook so that we can always look back at the guideposts of our journey, both as individuals and together. In the weeks leading up to my birthday, we'd traveled together, we'd been apart for a week, we'd thrown an event together in which we remained super connected as we enjoyed fluidity with others, we'd had a beautifully kinky date with a new couple friend down the road ... the list goes on. With the little square pinched between my fingers, I looked at Itai and said, "My intention today is to believe *in my body* that I get to have the life I want."

He smiled and said, "My intention today is to really see whatever you want to show me."

The next eight hours became a meditation on just how good it already was. It seemed every few minutes I was overcome with gratitude for a different aspect of my life.

The home we built together was a cozy nest of my favorite colors, textures, and smells, with a man I loved always cooking for me, excited to feed me. Prioritizing play and creativity and togetherness in this space had helped me shift from looking for what's wrong to a full-body exhale.

My work felt inspired and expansive. Learning to center pleasure in my client interactions and how I implemented business systems offered me a sense of purpose I couldn't imagine living without.

Friendships had emerged that were more profound than I knew possible.

Communicating through conflict and deepening understanding of each other, Itai and I had developed an unshakable foundation. Allowing each other to have big feelings and learning how to tend to them without overriding them had helped us root into the unique connection of *our* intimacy.

I had experienced so much more pleasure in my body than I'd dreamed possible, and knew that all the new people I was dating and exploring with were opportunities to get to know new forms of my own expression and enjoyment of life.

Itai and I strolled down the dirt road next to our house, marveling at a sky that seemed designed specifically for whatever weirdos decided to make it an acid Sunday and I realized that what made it at all even better was that I really had created it. The joy I'd finally found wasn't a product of simply allowing things to unfold, but of mustering the agency to claim my pleasure no matter how painful circumstances became. It struck me that I had actually already created a life my younger self never even knew to dream of. All it took to believe it in my body was a little bit of orienting.

When we closed the trip that evening I wrote, "I feel it! In my body! I already have the life I want *and* I get to keep building it."

You can have the relationships you want, and they will support the life you want. You can have the security of a partnership that operates as a rock-solid team while you fuck your brains out with other people, if that's what you want. You can develop deep, ongoing, supportive relationships with multiple people at once, who also adore each other, if that's what you want. The magic key is actually knowing what you want, learning to listen for where and how and when your conditioned mind distorts the messages from your body before the body's true desires are lost.

RECOMMENDED RESOURCES

- *Polysecure* by Jessica Fern
- *ReBloom: Archetypal Trauma Resolution for Personal & Collective Healing* by Rachael Maddox
- *In an Unspoken Voice: How the Body Releases Trauma and Restores Goodness* by Peter Levine
- *Pleasure Activism: The Politics of Feeling Good* by adrienne maree brown
- *Open Deeply: A Guide to Building Conscious, Compassionate Open Relationships* by Kate Loree, LMFT
- *Polyamory and Parenthood* by the Daylovers

ACKNOWLEDGMENTS

For me, there is no greater gift than realizing I belong. Writing this book has transformed my sense of belonging, and there are so many, many gratitudes I need to express;

First to Dad, who laid the groundwork for me to write and told me it was always OK to get more books. And who I kind of hope doesn't read this...

To the giant thinkers who came before me, the teachers who have graced my life, and the colleagues I am increasingly excited to find myself amongst.

To my clients, who are brave beyond reason, particularly when things are overwhelming and raw. It's thanks to your willingness to show up that I get to live my purpose (and that this book makes any sense). Each and every session leaves me humbled and inspired.

To Lauren Marie Flemming, Finn, Mars, Jess, and Ana and the Write Your Friggin' Book Already Community for holding me as I got the ball rolling. For mirroring the acceptance we all need in order to do hard things.

To Angela Lauria, Natasa Smirnov, and everybody at the Author Incubator for guiding me to a new version of myself. You will forever have my most profound gratitude for making me feel like I could trust you with this content and my process. My ADHD especially thanks you for all the clear, specific, broken-down to-do lists. Natasa, your ability to see me so quickly, and to be the wise carrot-dangling editor that you are made this book possible. I couldn't have dreamed for someone to make me feel safer than you did while I flailed and freaked out along the way.

To my witches in Pleasure Coven, and the cubs of Curiosity Bears, for enriching my life in more ways than I can count, and constantly reminding me to trust the things that I create. You have all shown me so much about the goodness in life. Your trust means the world to me.

To Lynne, for the skilled guidance living in my own body.

To Bear, Amelia and Che Che, each of whom have championed different parts of my work. Each of you holds their own dear, special place in my heart.

To Margeaux, for the sweet, delicate balance of friendship and work collaboration, both of which have been such delightful, expansive gifts.

To my various pockets of cheerleaders, friends, lovers, and chosen fam; Merissa, Adam, Anna, Alex, Cam, Amanda, Ru, Cassie, Andy, Dave, Abby, Dena, David, Charlie, Lizzie, Rasha, Joel, Vicki, Seann, William, Tsleel, Devon, Jeremy, Jess, Erin, Jean-Francois, Lindsay, Ayesha, and Miles. I can't begin to describe what a difference each of you have made in my life simply by being you.

To everyone who interacted with my procrastination in North Hollywood. Edoe, Amir, Stormy, thanks for all your graciousness. But Edoe, special thanks for all the time spent gassing me up.

To Kiki, you motherfucking godsend of an angel dime piece. I didn't believe in manifestation until that fateful night in September... There are no words to adequately address your generosity. Truly, I hope we get to poolside sob about liberation for the rest of our lives.

To Rachael, for the invitation, the friendship, and the unbridled genius-sharing. And also for having the boundaries to say, "I'm not your girl. Talk to Angela."

To Bess, what do I even say? Thank you for all the mirroring, for not having an off button when we're together, and for building the outside-the-box-intimacy we both know won't go anywhere. I can't imagine this phase of life without our partnership. I'll try not to make you drive cross-country in a stick shift ever again.

To Kristi, thinking of you forces me to confront how funny it is to be a writer obsessed with embodiment; words can't touch how my body feels about our relationship. Your support has been invaluable.

And finally, Itai, I could fill another whole book with just my gratitude for you. Nobody knows better than you what it took for me to get here. This book would not exist without your love and support, and all the times you fed me when I thought staring at a blank computer screen was so important. Your care has transformed my life. I know our collaboration will continue to guide my evolution, and there is nothing that brings me more peace than that knowing. Thank you for a life of true partnership.

ABOUT THE AUTHOR

 Irene Morning (she / her) is a somatic pleasure coach, intimacy educator, and polyamorous femme who has helped countless people transform from triggered and anxious to empowered and fulfilled. Passionate about the possibilities for healing through relationships, Irene is both a devoted student and facilitator of human connection. From her own experience, as well as the miracles she's seen in her work, she believes not only do we deserve to live the lives we want, but also that we are perfectly capable of creating them.

In addition to her private coaching practice, she is the founder and creator of Pleasure Coven (an ongoing group program for femmes reclaiming pleasure) as well as Vice President / Managing Director of Curiosity Bears (a sex-positive events community based in Southern California). As a result, Irene gratefully remains in awe of the powers of pleasure to alchemize trauma and facilitate liberation.

Drawing from a Master of Science from Maryland University of Integrative Health, a bachelor's degree focused on social theory, and thousands of hours of supervision, and experience in both somatic healing and sexual health counseling (via Planned Parenthood, Institute for Sexuality Education & Enlightenment, and Health Imperatives), Irene weaves together a rich tapestry of complementary sciences to advance the art of human relating.

When she's not busy working, you'll find Irene exploring her own pleasure. That includes cuddling on the couch, making flower arrangements, eating ice cream cones, and taking daily sunset walks. Her favorite thing is the shade of pink that fills the sky at dusk in the desert she calls home, the place of stolen Yuhaaviatam / Maarenga'yam land (otherwise called Joshua Tree, California).

Website: http://irenemorning.com
E-mail: irene@irenemorning.com
Instagram: @irene_morning

GIFT FOR READERS

As a thank you for reading, and to help you embody what we've talked about here, I made you something! Chapter 4 talked about regulation tools and Chapter 6 talked about pleasure as a resource for regulating. In this 30-minute class, we combine the two as I walk you through identifying the pleasure practices that are most supportive to *your* specific regulation. Just go to https://www.irenemorn ing.com/polyparadoxgift to download your free gift.

Printed in Great Britain
by Amazon